Hong Kong Trust Laws

International Law & Taxation Publishers

London

Hong Kong Trust Laws

ISBN 1-893713-20-2

Copyright © 2001 International Law & Taxation Publishers

International Law & Taxation Publishers
London

http://www.internationallawandtaxationpublishers.com

Contents

TRUSTEE ORDINANCE

CHAPTER 29

CONTENTS

Part I - Preliminary

Part II - Investments

Part III - General Powers of Trustees and Personal Representatives

General Powers

Part IX - General Provisions

CHAPTER 29

TRUSTEE

To amend the law relating to trustees.

PART I - Preliminary

Short title

1.   This Ordinance may be cited as the Trustee Ordinance.

Interpretation

2.   In this Ordinance, unless the context otherwise requires-

"authorized investments" means investments authorized by the instrument, if any, creating the trust for the investment of money subject to the trust, or by law;

"contingent right" as applied to land includes a contingent or executory interest, a possibility coupled with an interest, whether the object of the gift or limitation of the interest of possibility is or is not ascertained, also a right of entry, whether immediate or future, and whether vested or contingent;

"convey" and "conveyance" as applied to any person include the execution by that person of every necessary or suitable assurance (including an assent) for conveying, assigning, appointing, surrendering, or otherwise transferring or disposing of land whereof he is seized or possessed, or wherein he is entitled to a contingent right, either for his whole estate or for any less estate, together with the performance of all formalities required by law for the validity of the conveyance;

"income" includes rents and profits;

"instrument" includes enactment;

"land" includes land of any tenure, and mines and minerals, whether or not severed from the surface, buildings or parts of buildings, whether the division is horizontal, vertical or made in any other way, and other corporeal hereditaments; also a rent and other incorporeal hereditaments, and an easement, right, privilege, or benefit in, over, or derived from land, or an undivided share in land; and in this definition "mines and minerals" includes any strata or seam of minerals or substances in or under any land, and powers of working and getting the same, and an undivided share thereof;

5

"lunatic" means any person who has been found by due course of law to be of unsound mind and incapable of managing his affairs;

"mortgage" and "mortgagee" include and relate to every estate and interest regarded in equity as merely a security for money, and every person deriving title under the original mortgagee;

"pay" and "payment" as applied in relation to stocks and securities and in connexion with the expression "into court" include the deposit or transfer of the same in or into court;

"person of unsound mind" means any person, not a minor, who not having been found to be a lunatic is incapable from infirmity of mind of managing his own affairs;

"personal representative" means the executor, original or by representation, or administrator for the time being of a deceased person;

"possession" includes receipt of rents and profits or the right to receive the same, if any; and "possessed" applies to receipt of income of and to any vested estate less than a life interest in possession or in expectancy in any land;

"property" includes movable and immovable property, and any estate, share and interest in any property, movable or immovable, and any debt, and anything in action, and any other right or interest, whether in possession or not;

"rights" includes estates and interests;

"sale" includes an exchange;

"securities" includes stocks, funds and shares, and so far as relates to payments into court has the same meaning as in the enactments relating to funds in court and "securities payable to bearer" includes securities transferable by delivery or by delivery and endorsement;

"stock" includes fully paid up shares, and, so far as relates to vesting orders made by the court under this Ordinance, includes any fund, annuity, or security transferable in books kept by any corporation, company or society, or by instrument of transfer either alone or accompanied by other formalities, and any share or interest therein;

"transfer", in relation to stock or securities, includes the performance and execution of every deed, power of attorney, act, and thing on the part of the transferor to effect and complete the title in the transferee;

"trust" does not include the duties incident to an estate conveyed by way of mortgage, but with this exception the expression "trust" and "trustee" extend to implied and constructive trusts, and to cases where the trustee has a beneficial interest in the trust property, and to the duties incident to the office of a personal representative, and "trustee" where the context admits includes a personal representative, and "new trustee" includes an additional trustee;

"trust corporation" means the Public Trustee in England or a corporation appointed by the court in any particular case to be a trustee (if authorized by its constitution to act as trustee) or any trust company registered under Part VIII;

"trust for sale", in relation to land, means an immediate binding trust for sale, whether or not exercisable at the request or with the consent of any person, and with or without power at discretion to postpone the sale; and

"trustees for sale" means the persons (including a personal representative) holding land on trust for sale.

Application

3.(1) This Ordinance, except where otherwise expressly provided, applies to trusts including, so far as this Ordinance applies thereto, executorships and administratorships constituted or created either before or after the commencement of this Ordinance.

(2) The powers conferred by this Ordinance on trustees are in addition to the powers conferred by the instrument, if any, creating the trust, but those powers, unless otherwise stated, apply if and so far only as a contrary intention is not expressed in the instrument, if any, creating the trust, and have effect subject to the terms of that instrument.

(3) This Ordinance does not affect the legality or validity of anything done before the commencement of this Ordinance, except as otherwise expressly provided.

PART II - Investments

Authorized investments

4.(1) A trustee may invest any trust funds in his hands, whether at the time in a state of investment or not-

      (a)   in any investment specified in the Second Schedule;

      (b)   in any other investment (including deposits in a bank outside Hong Kong) which may be authorized by the court on summary application for that purpose made in chambers.

(2) Any application to the court made under subsection (1)(b) shall be made by the trustee ex parte and shall be supported by affidavit.

(3) The Financial Secretary may from time to time by order published in the Gazette amend the Second Schedule.

Retention of redeemable stocks until redemption

5. A trustee may retain until redemption any redeemable stock, fund, or security which may have been purchased in accordance with the powers of this Ordinance, or any Ordinance replaced by this Ordinance.

Discretion of trustees

6. Every power conferred by sections 4 and 5 shall be exercised according to the discretion of the trustee, but subject to any consent or direction with respect to the investment of the trust funds, required by the instrument, if any, creating the trust or by any Ordinance.

Retention of unauthorized investment

7. A trustee shall not be liable for breach of trust by reason only of his continuing to hold an investment which has ceased to be an investment authorized by the trust instrument or by the general law.

Investment in bearer securities

8.(1) A trustee may, unless expressly prohibited by the instrument creating the trust, retain or invest in securities payable to bearer which, if not so payable, would have been authorized investments.

(2) Securities payable to bearer retained or taken as an investment by a trustee (not being a trust corporation) shall, until sold, be deposited by him for safe custody and collection of income with a banker or banking company.

(3) A direction that investments shall be retained or made in the name of a trustee shall not, for the purposes of this section, be deemed to be such an express prohibition as aforesaid.

(4) A trustee shall not be responsible for any loss incurred by reason of such deposit, and any sum payable in respect of such deposit and collection shall be paid out of the income of the trust property.

Loans and investments by trustees not chargeable as breaches of trust

9.(1) A trustee lending money on the security of any property on which he can properly lend shall not be chargeable with breach of trust by reason only of the proportion borne by the amount of the loan to the value of the property at the time when the loan was made, if it appears to the court-

> *(a)* that immediately prior to the making of the loan the trustee obtained a report as to the value of the property made by a person whom he reasonably believed to be an able practical surveyor or valuer instructed and employed independently of any owner of the property, whether such surveyor or valuer carried on business in the locality where the property is situate or elsewhere; and

> *(b)* that the amount of the loan does not exceed one half of the value of the property as stated in the report; and

> *(c)* that the loan was made under the advice of the surveyor or valuer expressed in the report.

(2) A trustee lending money on the security of any leasehold property shall not be chargeable with breach of trust only upon the ground that in making such loan he dispensed either wholly or partly with the production or investigation of the lessor's title.

(3) A trustee shall not be chargeable with breach of trust only upon the ground that in effecting the purchase, or in lending money upon the security, of any property he has accepted a shorter title than the title which a purchaser is, in the absence of a special contract, entitled to require, if in the opinion of the court the title accepted be such as a person acting with prudence and caution would have accepted.

(4) This section applies to transfers of existing securities as well as to new securities and to investments made before as well as after the commencement of this Ordinance.

Liability for loss by reason of improper investment

10.(1) Where a trustee improperly advances trust money on a mortgage security which would at the time of the investment be a proper investment in all respects for a smaller sum than is actually advanced thereon, the security shall be deemed an authorized investment for the smaller sum, and the trustee shall only be liable to make good the sum advanced in excess thereof with interest.

(2) This section applies to investments made before as well as after the commencement of this Ordinance.

Powers supplementary to powers of investment

11.(1) Trustees lending money on the security of any property on which they can lawfully lend may contract that such money shall not be called in during any period not exceeding 7 years from the time when the loan was made, provided interest be paid within a specified time not exceeding 30 days after every half-yearly or other day on which it becomes due, and provided there be no breach of any covenant by the mortgagor contained in the instrument of mortgage or charge for the maintenance and protection of the property.

(2) On a sale by trustees of land for a term having at least 60 years to run, the trustees may, where the proceeds are liable to be invested, contract that the payment of any part, not exceeding two-thirds, of the purchase money shall be secured by mortgage of the land sold, with or without the security of any other property, but such mortgage, if any buildings are comprised therein, shall contain a covenant by the mortgagor to keep such buildings insured against loss or damage by fire to the full value thereof.

(3) The trustees shall not be bound to obtain any report as to the value of the land or other property to be comprised in such mortgage, or any advice as to the making of the loan, and shall not be liable for any loss which may be incurred by reason only of the security being insufficient at the date of the mortgage.

(4) Where any securities of a company are subject to a trust, the trustees may concur in any scheme or arrangement-

> *(a)* for the reconstruction of the company;
>
> *(b)* for the sale of all or any part of the property and undertaking of the company to another company;
>
> *(c)* for the amalgamation of the company with another company;
>
> *(d)* for the release, modification, or variation of any rights, privileges or liabilities attached to the securities or any of them,

in like manner as if they were entitled to such securities beneficially, with power to accept any securities of any denomination or description of the reconstructed or purchasing or new company in lieu of or in exchange for all or any of the first-mentioned securities; and the trustees shall not be responsible for any loss occasioned by any act or thing so done in good faith, and may retain any securities so accepted as aforesaid for any period for which they could have properly retained the original securities.

(5) If any conditional or preferential right to subscribe for any securities in any company is offered to trustees in respect of any holding in such company, they may as to all or any of such securities, either exercise such right and apply capital money subject to the trust in payment of the consideration, or renounce such right, or assign for the best consideration that can be reasonably obtained the benefit of such right or the title thereto to any person, including any beneficiary under the trust, without being responsible for any loss occasioned by any act or thing so done by them in good faith:

Provided that the consideration for any such assignment shall be held as capital money of the trust.

(6) The powers conferred by this section shall be exercisable subject to the consent of any person whose consent to a change of investment is required by law or by the instrument, if any, creating the trust.

(7) Where the loan referred to in subsection (1), or the sale referred to in subsection (2), is made under the order of the court, the powers conferred by those subsections respectively shall apply only if and as far as the court may by order direct.

Power to deposit at bank and to pay calls

12.(1) Trustees may, pending the negotiation and preparation of any mortgage or charge, or during any other time while an investment is being sought for, pay any trust money into a bank to a deposit or other account, and all interest, if any, payable in respect thereof shall be applied as income.

(2) Trustees may apply capital money subject to a trust in payment of the calls on any shares subject to the same trust.

PART III- General Powers of Trustees and Personal Representatives

General Powers
Power of trustees for sale to sell by auction, etc.

13.(1) Where a trust for sale or a power of sale of property is vested in a trustee, he may sell or concur with any other person in selling all or any part of the property, either subject to prior charges or not, and either together or in lots, by public auction or by private contract, subject to any such conditions respecting title or evidence of title or other matter as the trustee thinks fit, with power to vary any contract for sale, and to buy in at any auction, or to rescind any contract for sale and to resell, without being answerable for any loss.

(2) A trust or power to sell or dispose of land includes a trust or power to sell or dispose of part thereof, whether the division is horizontal, vertical, or made in any other way.

Power to sell subject to depreciatory conditions

14.(1) No sale made by a trustee shall be impeached by any beneficiary upon the ground that any of the conditions subject to which the sale was made may have been unnecessarily depreciatory, unless it also appears that the consideration for the sale was thereby rendered inadequate.

(2) No sale made by a trustee shall, after the execution of the conveyance, be impeached as against the purchaser upon the ground that any of the conditions subject to which the sale was made may have been unnecessarily depreciatory, unless it appears that the purchaser was acting in collusion with the trustee at the time when the contract for sale was made.

(3) No purchaser, upon any sale made by a trustee, shall be at liberty to make any objection against the title upon any of the grounds aforesaid.

(4) This section applies to sales made before or after the commencement of this Ordinance.

Power of trustees to give receipts

15.(1) The receipt in writing of a trustee for any money, securities, or other personal property or effects payable, transferable, or deliverable to him under any trust or power shall be a sufficient discharge to the person paying, transferring, or delivering the same and shall effectually exonerate him from seeing to the application or being answerable for any loss or misapplication thereof.

(2) A receipt in writing for the proceeds of sale or other capital money arising under a trust for sale of land shall be a sufficient discharge if it is signed by the person or persons lawfully executing the conveyance in pursuance of that sale and the person making payment shall not be liable for any loss or misapplication of those proceeds or that money.

(3) This section applies notwithstanding anything to the contrary in the instrument, if any, creating the trust.

Power to do other acts

16. A personal representative, or 2 or more trustees acting together, or, subject to the restrictions imposed in regard to receipts by a sole trustee not being a trust corporation, a sole acting trustee where by the instrument, if any, creating the trust, or by statute, a sole trustee is authorized to execute the trusts and powers reposed in him, may, if and as he or they think fit-

> *(a)* accept any property, before the time at which it is made transferable or payable; or

> *(b)* sever and apportion any blended trust funds or property; or

> *(c)* pay or allow any debt or claim on any evidence that he or they think sufficient; or

> *(d)* accept any composition or any security, for any debt, or for any property, claimed; or

> *(e)* allow any time for payment of any debt; or

> *(f)* compromise, compound, abandon, submit to arbitration, or otherwise settle any debt, account, claim, or thing whatever relating to the testator's or intestate's estate or to the trust,

and for any of those purposes may enter into, give, execute and do such agreements, instruments or composition or arrangement, releases, and other things as to him or them seem expedient, without being responsible for any loss occasioned by any act or thing so done by him or them in good faith.

Powers of trustees of renewable leaseholds to renew and raise money for the purpose

17.(1) A trustee of any leaseholds for lives or years which are renewable from time to time either under any covenant or contract, or by custom or usual practice, may, if he thinks fit, and shall, if thereto required by any person having any beneficial interest, present or future, or contingent, in the leaseholds, use his best endeavours to obtain from time to time a renewed lease of the same hereditaments on the accustomed and reasonable terms, and for that purpose may from time to time make or concur in making a surrender of the lease for the time being subsisting, and do all such other acts as are requisite:

Provided that, where by the terms of the settlement or will the person in possession for his life or other limited interest is entitled to enjoy the same without any obligation to renew or to contribute to the expense of renewal, this section shall not apply unless the consent in writing of that person is obtained to the renewal on the part of the trustee.

(2) If money is required to pay for the renewal, the trustee effecting the renewal may pay the same out of any money then in his hands in trust for the persons beneficially interested in the lands to be comprised in the renewal lease, and if he has not in his hands sufficient money for the purpose he may raise the money required by mortgage of the hereditaments to be comprised in the renewed lease, or of any other hereditaments for the time being subject to the uses or trusts to which those hereditaments are subject, and no person advancing money upon a mortgage purporting to be under this power shall be bound to see that the money is wanted, or that no more is raised than is wanted for the purpose, or otherwise as to the application thereof.

(3) This section applies to trusts created either before or after the commencement of this Ordinance, but nothing in this section shall authorize any trustee to do anything which he is in express terms forbidden to do, or to omit to do anything which he is in express terms directed to do, by the instrument creating the trust.

Power to raise money by sale, mortgage, etc.

18.(1) Where trustees are authorized by the instrument, if any, creating the trust or by law to pay or apply capital money subject to the trust for any purpose or in any manner, they shall have and shall be deemed always to have had power to raise the money required by sale, conversion, calling in, or mortgage of all or any part of the trust property for the time being inpossession.

(2) This section applies notwithstanding anything to the contrary contained in the instrument, if any, creating the trust, but does not apply to trustees of property held for charitable purposes.

Protection to purchasers and mortgagees
dealing with trustees

19. No purchaser or mortgagee, paying or advancing money on a sale or mortgage purporting to be made under any trust or power vested in trustees, shall be concerned to see that such money is wanted, or that no more than is wanted is raised, or otherwise as to the application thereof.

Devolution of powers or trusts

20.(1) Where a power or trust is given to or imposed on 2 or more trustees jointly, the same may be exercised or performed by the survivors or survivor ofthem for the time being.

(2) Until the appointment of new trustees, the personal representatives or representative for the time being of a sole trustee, or, where there were 2 or more trustees of the last surviving or continuing trustee, shall be capable of exercising or performing any power or trust which was given to, or capable of being exercised by, the sole or last surviving or continuing trustee, or other the trustees or trustee for the time being of the trust.

(3) This section takes effect subject to the restrictions imposed in regard to receipts by a sole trustee, not being a trust corporation.

(4) In this section "personal representative" does not include an executor who has renounced or has not proved.

Power to insure

21.(1) A trustee may insure against loss or damage by fire and typhoon any building or other insurable property to any amount, including the amount of any insurance already on foot, up to the full value of the building or property, and pay the premiums for such insurance out of the income thereof or out of the income of any other property subject to the same trusts without obtaining the consent of any person who may be entitled wholly or partly to such income.

(2) This section does not apply to any building or property which a trustee is bound forthwith to convey absolutely to any beneficiary upon being requested to do so.

Application of insurance money where policy kept up under any trust, power or obligation

22.(1) Money receivable by trustees or any beneficiary under a policy of insurance against the loss or damage of any property subject to a trust, whether by fire or otherwise, shall, where the policy has been kept up under any trust in that behalf or under any power statutory or otherwise, or in performance of any covenant or of any obligation statutory or otherwise, or by a tenant for life impeachable for waste, be capital money for the purpose of the trust as the case may be.

(2) If any such money is receivable by any person, other than the trustees of the trust, that person shall use his best endeavours to recover and receive the money, and shall pay the net residue thereof after discharging any costs of recovering and receiving it, to the trustees of the trust, or, if there are no trustees capable of giving a discharge therefor, into court.

(3) Any such money-

> *(a)*   if it was receivable in respect of property held upon trust for sale, shall be held upon the trusts and subject to the powers and provisions applicable to money arising by a sale under such trust;

> *(b)*   in any other case, shall be held upon trusts corresponding as nearly as may be with the trusts affecting the property in respect of which it was payable.

(4) Such money, or any part thereof, may also be applied by the trustees, or, if in court, under the direction of the court, in rebuilding, reinstating, replacing, or repairing the property lost or damaged, but any such application by the trustees shall be subject to the consent of any person whose consent is required by the instrument, if any, creating the trust to the investment of money subject to the trust.

(5) Nothing contained in this section shall prejudice or affect the right of any person to require any such money or any part thereof to be applied in rebuilding, reinstating, or repairing the property lost or damaged, or the right of any mortgagee, lessor, or lessee, whether under any statute or otherwise.

(6) This section applies to policies effected either before or after the commencement of this Ordinance, but only to money received after such commencement.

Deposit of documents for safe custody

23. Trustees may deposit any documents held by them relating to the trust, or to the trust property, with any banker or banking company or any other company whose business includes the undertaking of the safe custody of documents, and any sum payable in respect of such deposit shall be paid out of the income of the trust property.

Reversionary interests, valuations, and audit

24.(1) Where trust property includes any share or interest in property not vested in the trustees, or the proceeds of sale of any such property, or any other thing in action, the trustees on the same falling into possession, or becoming payable or transferable may-

> *(a)*   agree or ascertain the amount or value thereof or any part thereof in such manner as they may think fit;

> *(b)*   accept in or towards satisfaction thereof, at the market or current value, or upon any valuation or estimate of value which they may think fit, any authorized investments;

> *(c)*   allow any deductions for duties, costs, charges and expenses which they may think proper or reasonable;

> *(d)*   execute any release in respect of the premises so as effectually to discharge all accountable parties from all liability in respect of any matters coming within the scope of such release,

without being responsible in any such case for any loss occasioned by any act or thing so done by them in good faith.

(2) The trustees shall not be under any obligation and shall not be chargeable with any breach of trust by reason of any omission-

> *(a)*   to apply for any stop or other like order upon any securities or other property out of or on which such share or interest or other thing in action as aforesaid is derived, payable or charged; or

> *(b)*   to take any proceedings on account of any act, default, or neglect on the part of the persons in whom such securities or other property or any of them or any part thereof are for the time being, or had at any time been, vested,

unless and until required in writing so to do by some person, or the guardian of some person, beneficially interested under the trust, and unless also due provision is made to their satisfaction for payment of the costs of any proceedings required to be taken:

Provided that nothing in this subsection shall relieve the trustees of the obligation to get in and obtain payment or transfer of such share or interest or other thing in action on the same falling into possession.

(3) Trustees may, for the purpose of giving effect to the trust, or any of the provisions of the instrument, if any, creating the trust or of any statute, from time to time (by duly qualified agents) ascertain and fix the value of any trust property in such manner as they think proper, and any valuation so made in good faith shall be binding upon all persons interested under the trust.

(4) Trustees may, in their absolute discretion, from time to time, but not more than once in every year unless the nature of the trust or any special dealings with the trust property make a more frequent exercise of the right reasonable, cause the accounts of the trust property to be examined or audited by an independent accountant, and shall, for that purpose, produce such vouchers and give such information to him as he may require; and the costs of such examination or audit, including the fee of the auditor, shall be paid out of the capital or income of the trust property, or partly in one way and partly in the other as the trustees, in their absolute discretion, think fit, but, in default of any direction by the trustees to the contrary in any special case, costs attributable to capital shall be borne by capital and those attributable to income by income.

Power to employ agents

25.(1) Trustees or personal representatives may, instead of acting personally, employ and pay an agent, whether a solicitor, banker, stockbroker, or other person, to transact any business or do any act required to be transacted or done in the execution of the trust, or the administration of the testator's or intestate's estate, including the receipt and payment of money, and shall be entitled to be allowed and paid all charges and expenses so incurred, and shall not be responsible for the default of any such agent if employed in good faith.

(2) Trustees or personal representatives may appoint any person to act as their agent or attorney for the purpose of selling, converting, collecting, getting in, and executing and perfecting insurances of, or managing or cultivating, or otherwise administering any property, movable or immovable, subject to the trust or forming part of the testator's or intestate's estate, in any place outside Hong Kong, or executing or exercising any discretion or trust or power vested in them in relation to any such property, with such ancillary powers, and with and subject to such provisions and restrictions as they may think fit, including a power to appoint substitutes, and shall not, by reason only of their having made such appointment, be responsible for any loss arising thereby.

(3) Without prejudice to such general power of appointing agents as aforesaid-

    (a)   a trustee may appoint a solicitor to be his agent to receive and

give a discharge for any money or valuable consideration or property receivable by the trustee under the trust, by permitting the solicitor to have the custody of, and to produce, a deed having in the body thereof or endorsed thereon a receipt for such money or valuable consideration or property, the deed being executed, or the endorsed receipt being signed, by the person entitled to give a receipt for that consideration;

(b) a trustee shall not be chargeable with breach of trust by reason only of his having made or concurred in making any such appointment; and the production of any such deed by the solicitor shall have the same statutory validity and effect as if the person appointing the solicitor had not been a trustee;

(c) a trustee may appoint a banker or solicitor to be his agent to receive and give a discharge for any money payable to the trustee under or by virtue of a policy of insurance, by permitting the banker or solicitor to have the custody of and to produce the policy of insurance with a receipt signed by the trustee, and a trustee shall not be chargeable with a breach of trust by reason only of his having made or concurred in making any such appointment:

Provided that nothing in this subsection shall exempt a trustee from any liability which he would have incurred if this Ordinance and any enactment replaced by this Ordinance had not been passed, in case he permits any such money, valuable consideration, or property to remain in the hands or under the control of the banker or solicitor for a period longer than is reasonably necessary to enable the banker or solicitor, as the case may be, to pay or transfer the same to the trustee. This subsection applies whether the money or valuable consideration or property was or is received before or after the commencement of this Ordinance.

Power to concur with others

26. Where an undivided share in the proceeds of sale of land directed to be sold, or in any other property, is subject to a trust, or forms part of the estate of a testator or intestate, the trustees or personal representatives may (without prejudice to the trust for sale affecting the entirety of the land and the powers of the trustees for sale in reference thereto) execute or exercise any trust or power vested in them in relation to such share in conjunction with the persons entitled to or having power in that half over the other share or shares, and notwithstanding that any one or more of the trustees or personal representatives may be entitled to or interested in any such other share, either in his or their own right or in a fiduciary capacity.

Power to delegate trusts

27.(1) Notwithstanding any rule of law or equity to the contrary, a trustee may, by power of attorney, delegate for a period not exceeding 12 months the execution or exercise of all or any of the trusts, powers and discretions vested in him as trustee either alone or jointly with any other person or persons.

(2) The persons who may be donees of a power of attorney under this section include a trust corporation but not (unless a trust corporation) the only other co-trustee of the donor of the power.

(3) An instrument creating a power of attorney under this section shall beattested by at least one witness.

(4) Before or within 7 days after giving a power of attorney under this section the donor shall give written notice thereof (specifying the date on which the power comes into operation and its duration, the donee of the power, the reason why the power is given and, where some only are delegated, the trusts, powers and discretions delegated) to -

> *(a)* each person (other than himself) if any, who under any instrument creating the trust has power (whether alone or jointly) to appoint a new trustee; and

> *(b)* each of the other trustees, if any,

but failure to comply with this subsection shall not, in favour of a person dealing with the donee of the power, invalidate any act done or instrument executed by the donee.

(5) The donor of a power of attorney given under this section shall be liable for acts or defaults of the donee in the same manner as if they were the acts or defaults of the donor.

(6) For the purpose of executing or exercising the trusts or powers delegated to him, the donee may exercise any of the powers conferred on the donor as trustee by statute or by the instrument creating the trust, including power, for the purpose of the transfer of any inscribed stock, himself to delegate to an attorney power to transfer but not including the power of delegation conferred by this section.

(7) The fact that it appears from any power of attorney given under this section, or from any evidence required for the purposes of any such power of attorney or otherwise, that in dealing with any stock the donee of the power isacting in the execution of a trust shall not be deemed for any purpose to affect any person in whose books the stock is inscribed or registered with any notice of the trust.

(8) This section applies-

> *(a)* to a personal representative as it applies to a trustee except that subsection (4) shall apply as if it required notice there mentioned to be given to each of the other personal

representatives, if any, except any executor who has renounced probate;

(b) whenever the trusts, powers or discretions in question arose.

Indemnities

Protection against liability in respect of rents and covenants

28.(1) Where a personal representative or trustee liable as such for-

(a) any rent, covenant, or agreement reserved by or contained in any lease; or

(b) any rent, covenant or agreement payable under or contained in any grant made in consideration of a rent charge; or

(c) any indemnity given in respect of any rent, covenant or agreement referred to in either of the foregoing paragraphs,

satisfies all liabilities under the lease or grant which may have accrued, and been claimed, up to the date of the conveyance hereinafter mentioned, and, where necessary, sets apart a sufficient fund to answer any future claim that may be made in respect of any fixed and ascertained sum which the lessee or grantee agreed to lay out on the property demised or granted, although the period for laying out the same may not have arrived, then and in any such case the personal representative or trustee may convey the property demised or granted to a purchaser, legatee, devisee or other person entitled to call for a conveyance thereof and thereafter-

(i) he may distribute the residuary estate of the deceased testator or intestate, or, as the case may be, the trust estate (other than the fund, if any, set apart as aforesaid) to or amongst the persons entitled thereto, without appropriating any part, or any further part, as the case may be, of the estate of the deceased or of the trust estate to meet any future liability under the said lease or grant;

(ii) notwithstanding such distribution, he shall not be personally liable in respect of any subsequent claim under the said lease or grant.

(2) This section operates without prejudice to the right of the lessor or grantor, or the persons deriving title under the lessor or grantor, to follow the assets of the deceased or the trust property into the hands of the persons amongst whom the same may have been respectively distributed, and applies notwithstanding anything to the contrary in the will or other instrument, if any, creating the trust.

(3) In this section "lease" includes an underlease and an agreement for a lease or underlease and any instrument giving any such indemnity as aforesaid or varying the liabilities under the lease; "grant" applies to a grant whether the rent is created by limitation, grant, reservation, or otherwise, and includes an agreement for a grant and any instrument giving any such indemnity as aforesaid or varying the liabilities under the grant; "lessee" and "grantee", include persons respectively deriving title under them.

Protection by means of advertisement

29.(1) With a view to the conveyance to or distribution among the persons entitled to any movable or immovable property, trustees or personal representatives may give notice by advertisement in the Gazette, and such other like notices, including notices elsewhere than in Hong Kong, as would, in any special case, have been directed by a court of competent jurisdiction in an action for administration, of their intention to make such conveyance or distribution as aforesaid, and requiring any person interested to send to the trustees or personal representatives within the time, not being less than 2 months, fixed in the notice or, where more than one notice is given, in the last of the notices, particulars of his claim in respect of the property or any part thereof to which the notice relates.

(2) At the expiration of the time fixed by the notice the trustees or personal representatives may convey or distribute the property or any part thereof to which the notice relates, to or among the persons entitled thereto, having regard only to the claims, whether formal or not, of which the trustees or personal representatives then had notice and shall not, as respects the property so conveyed or distributed, be liable to any person of whose claim the trustees or personal representatives have ot had notice at the time of conveyance or distribution; but nothing in this section shall-

> *(a)* prejudice the right of any person to follow the property, or any property representing the same, into the hands of any person, other than a purchaser, who may have received it; or

> *(b)* free the trustees or personal representatives from any obligation to make searches similar to those which an intending purchaser would be advised to make or obtain.

(3) This section applies notwithstanding anything to the contrary in the will or other instrument, if any, creating the trust.

Protection in regard to notice

30. A trustee or personal representative acting for the purposes of more than one trust or estate shall not, in the absence of fraud, by affected by notice of any instrument, matter, fact or thing in relation to any particular trust or estate if he has obtained notice thereof merely by reason of his acting or having acted for the purposes of another trust or estate.

31. *(Repealed)*

Implied indemnity of trustees

32.(1) A trustee shall be chargeable only for money and securities actually received by him notwithstanding his signing any receipt for the sake of conformity, and shall be answerable and accountable only for his own acts, receipts, neglects, or defaults, and not for those of any other trustee, or of any banker, broker, or other person with whom any trust money or securities may be deposited, nor for the insufficiency or deficiency of any securities, nor for any other loss, unless the same happens through his own wilful default.

(2) A trustee may reimburse himself or pay or discharge out of the trustpremises all expenses incurred in or about the execution of the trusts or powers.

Maintenance, Advancement and Protective Trusts
Power to apply income for maintenance and to accumulate
surplus income during a minority

33.(1) Where any property is held by trustees in trust for any person for any interest whatsoever, whether vested or contingent, then, subject to any prior interests or charges affecting that property-

> *(a)* during the infancy of any such person, if his interest so long continues, the trustees may, at their sole discretion, pay to his parent or guardian, if any, or otherwise apply for or towards his maintenance, education or benefit, the whole or such part, if any, of the income of that property as may, in all the circumstances, be reasonable, whether or not there is-
>
> > **(i)** any other fund applicable to the same purpose; or
> >
> > **(ii)** any person bound by law to provide for his maintenance or education; and
>
> *(b)* if such person on attaining full age has not a vested interest in such income, the trustees shall thenceforth pay the income of that property and of any accretion thereto under subsection (2) to him, until he either attains a vested interest therein or dies, or until failure of his interest:

Provided that, in deciding whether the whole or any part of the income of the property is during a minority to be paid or applied for the purposes aforesaid, the trustees shall have regard to the age of the infant and his requirements and generally to the circumstances of the case, and in particular to what other income, if any, is applicable for the same purposes; and where trustees have notice that the income of more than one fund is applicable for those purposes, then, so far as practicable, unless the entire income of the funds is paid or applied as aforesaid or the court otherwise directs, a proportionate part only of the income of each fund shall be so paid or applied.

(2) During the infancy of any such person, if his interest so long continues, the trustees shall accumulate all the residue of that income in the way of compound interest by investing the same and the resulting income thereof from time to time in authorized investments, and shall hold those accumulations as follows-

(a) if any such person-

(i) attains full age, or marries before attaining full age, and his interest in such income during his infancy or until his marriage is a vested interest; or

(ii) on attaining full age or on marriage before attaining full age becomes entitled to the property from which such income arose absolutely,

the trustees shall hold the accumulations in trust for such person absolutely, and so that the receipt of such person after marriage, and though still an infant, shall be a good discharge; and

(b) in any other case the trustees shall, notwithstanding that such person had a vested interest in such income, hold the accumulations as an accretion to the capital of the property from which such accumulations arose, and as one fund with such capital for all purposes,

but the trustees may, at any time during the infancy of such person if his interest so long continues, apply those accumulations, or any part thereof, as if they were income arising in the then current year.

(3) This section applies in the case of a contingent interest only if the limitation or trust carries the intermediate income of the property, but it applies to a future or contingent legacy by the parent of, or a person standing in loco parentis to, the legatee, if and for such period as, under the general law, the legacy carries interest for the maintenance of the legatee, and in any such case as last aforesaid the rate of interest shall (if the income available is sufficient, and subject to any rules of court to the contrary) be $5 per cent per annum.

(4) This section applies to a vested annuity in like manner as if the annuity were the income of property held by trustees in trust to pay the income thereof to the annuitant for the same period for which the annuity is payable, save that in any case accumulations made during the infancy of the annuitant shall be held in trust for the annuitant or his personal representatives absolutely.

(5) This section does not apply where the instrument, if any, under which the interest arises came into operation before the commencement of this Ordinance.

Power of advancement

34.(1) Trustees may at any time or times pay or apply any capital money subject to a trust, for the advancement or benefit in such manner as they may, in their absolute discretion, think fit, of any person entitled to the capital of the trust property or of any share thereof, whether absolutely or contingently on his attaining any specified age or on the occurrence of any other event, or subject to a gift over on his death under any specified age or on the occurrence of any other event, and whether in possession or in remainder or reversion, and such payment or application may be made notwithstanding that the interest of such person is liable to be defeated by the exercise of a power of appointment or revocation, or to be diminished by the increase of the class to which he belongs:

Provided that-

    (a)   the money so paid or applied for the advancement or benefit of any person shall not exceed altogether in amount one-half of the presumptive or vested share or interest of that person in the trust property; and

    (b)   if that person is or becomes absolutely and indefensibly entitled to a share in the trust property the money so paid or applied shall be brought into account as part of such share; and

    (c)   no such payment or application shall be made so as to prejudice any person entitled to any prior life or other interest, whether vested or contingent, in the money paid or applied unless such person is in existence and of full age and consents in writing to such payment or application.

(2) This section applies only where the trust property consists of money or securities or of property held upon trust for sale calling in and conversion, and such money or securities, or the proceeds of such sale calling in and conversion are not by statute or in equity considered as land.

(3) This section does not apply to trusts constituted or created before the commencement of this Ordinance.

Protective trusts

35.(1) Where any income, including an annuity or other periodical income payment, is directed to be held on protective trusts for the benefit of any person (in this section called the principal beneficiary) for the period of his life or for any less period, then, during the period (in this section called the trust period) the said income shall, without prejudice to any prior interest, be held on the following trusts, namely-

    (a)   upon trust for the principal beneficiary during the trust period or until he, whether before or after the termination of any prior interest, does or attempts to do or suffers any act or thing, or until any event happens, other than an advance under any

24

statutory or express power, whereby, if the said income were payable during the trust period to the principal beneficiary absolutely during that period, he would be deprived of the right to receive the same or any part thereof, in any of which cases, as well as on the termination of the trust period, whichever first happens, this trust of the said income shall fail or determine;

(b) if the trust aforesaid fails or determines during the subsistence of the trust period, then, during the residue of that period, the said income shall be held upon trust for the application thereof for the maintenance or support, or otherwise for the benefit, of all or any one or more exclusively of the other or others of the following persons (that is to say) -

(i) the principal beneficiary and his or her wife or husband, if any, and his or her children or more remote issue, if any; or

(ii) if there is no wife or husband or issue of the principal beneficiary in existence, the principal beneficiary and the persons who would, if he were actually dead, be entitled to the trust property or the income thereof or to the annuity fund, if any, or arrears of the annuity, as the case may be,

as the trustees in their absolute discretion, without being liable to account for the exercise of such discretion, think fit.

(2) This section does not apply to trusts coming into operation before the commencement of this Ordinance, and has effect subject to any variation of the implied trusts aforesaid contained in the instrument creating the trust.

(3) Nothing in this section operates to validate any trust which would, if contained in the instrument creating the trust, be liable to be set aside.

PART IV - Appointment and Discharge of Trustees

Limitation of the number of trustees

36.(1) Where, at the commencement of this Ordinance there are more than 4 trustees of a settlement of land or more than 4 trustees holding land on trust for sale, no new trustees shall (except where as a result of the appointment the number is reduced to 4 or less) be capable of being appointed until the number is reduced to less than 4, and thereafter the number shall not be increased beyond 4.

(2) In the case of settlements and dispositions on trust for sale of land made or coming into operation after the commencement of this Ordinance-

- *(a)* the number of trustees thereof shall not in any case exceed 4, and where more than 4 persons are named as such trustees, the 4 first named (who are able and willing to act) shall alone be the trustees, and the other persons named shall not be trustees unless appointed on the occurrence of a vacancy;

- *(b)* the number of the trustees shall not be increased beyond 4.

(3) The restrictions hereby imposed on the number of trustees do not apply in the case of land vested in trustees for charitable, ecclesiastical, or public purposes or where the net proceeds of the sale of the property are held for like purposes.

Power of appointing new or additional trustees

37.(1) Where a trustee, either original or substituted, and whether appointed by a court or otherwise, is dead, or remains out of Hong Kong for more than 12 months, or desires to be discharged from all or any of the trusts or powers reposed in or conferred on him, or refuses or is unfit to act therein, or is incapable of acting therein, or is a person under the age of 21 years, then, subject to the restrictions imposed by this Ordinance on the number of trustees-

- *(a)* the person or persons nominated for the purpose of appointing new trustees by the instrument, if any, creating the trust; or

- *(b)* if there is no such person, or no such person able and willing to act, then the surviving or continuing trustees or trustee for the time being, or the personal representatives of the last surviving or continuing trustee,

may, by writing, appoint one or more other persons (whether or not being the persons exercising the power) to be a trustee or trustees in the place of the trustee so deceased, remaining out of Hong Kong, desiring to be discharged, refusing, or being unfit or being incapable, or being a person under the age of 21 years, as aforesaid.

(2) Where a trustee has been removed under a power contained in the instrument creating the trust, a new trustee or new trustees may be appointed in the place of the trustee who is removed, as if he were dead, or, in the case of a corporation, as if the corporation desired to be discharged from the trust, and the provisions of this section shall apply accordingly, but subject to the restrictions imposed by this Ordinance on the number of trustees.

(3) Where a corporation being a trustee is or has been dissolved, either before or after the commencement of this Ordinance, then, for the purposes of this section and of any enactment replaced thereby, the corporation shall be deemed to be and to have been from the date of the dissolution incapable of acting in the trusts or powers reposed in or conferred on the corporation.

(4) The power of appointment given by subsection (1) or any similar previous enactment to the personal representatives of a last surviving or continuing trustee shall be and shall be deemed always to have been exercisable by the executors for the time being (whether original or by representation) of such surviving or continuing trustee who have proved the will of their testator or by the administrators for the time being of such trustee without the concurrence of any executor who has renounced or has not proved.

(5) But a sole or last surviving executor intending to renounce, or all the executors where they all intend to renounce, shall have and shall be deemed always to have had power, at any time before renouncing probate, to exercise the power of appointment given by this section, or by any similar previous enactment, if willing to act for that purpose and without thereby accepting the office of executor.

(6) Where a sole trustee, other than a trust corporation, is or has been originally appointed to act in a trust, or where, in the case of any trust, there are not more than 3 trustees (none of them being a trust corporation) either original or substituted and whether appointed by the court or otherwise, then and in any such case-

    (a)   the person or persons nominated for the purpose of appointing new trustees by the instrument, if any, creating the trust; or

    (b)   if there is no such person, or no such person able and willing to act, then the trustee or trustees for the time being,

may, by writing, appoint another person or other persons to be an additional trustee or additional trustees, but it shall not be obligatory to appoint any additional trustee, unless the instrument, if any, creating the trust, or any statutory enactment provides to the contrary, nor shall the number of trustees be increased beyond 4 by virtue of any such appointment.

(7) Every new trustee appointed under this section, as well before as after all the trust property becomes by law, or by assurance, or otherwise, vested in him, shall have the same powers, authorities, and discretions, and may in all respects act as if he had been originally appointed a trustee by the instrument, if any, creating the trust.

(8) The provisions of this section relating to a trustee who is dead include the case of a person nominated trustee in a will but dying before the testator,and those relative to a continuing trustee include a refusing or retiring trustee, if willing to act in the execution of the provisions of this section.

(9) Where a lunatic or person of unsound mind, being a trustee, is also entitled in possession to some beneficial interest in the trust property, no appointment of a new trustee in his place shall be made by the continuing trustees or trustee, under this section, unless leave has been given by the court to make the appointment.

Supplemental provisions as to appointment of trustees

38.(1) On the appointment of a trustee for the whole or any part of trust property-

(a) the number of trustees may, subject to the restrictions imposed by this Ordinance on the number of trustees, be increased; and

(b) a separate set of trustees, not exceeding 4 may be appointed for any part of the trust property held on trusts distinct from those relating to any other part or parts of the trust property, notwithstanding that no new trustees or trustee are or is to be appointed for other parts of the trust property, and any existing trustee may be appointed or remain one of such separate set of trustees, or, if only one trustee was originally appointed, then, save as hereinafter provided, one separate trustee may be appointed; and

(c) it shall not be obligatory, save as hereinafter provided, to appoint more than one new trustee where only one trustee was originally appointed, or to fill up the original number of trustees where more than 2 trustees were originally appointed, but, except where only one trustee was originally appointed, and a sole trustee when appointed will be able to give valid receipts for all capital money, a trustee shall not be discharged from his trust unless there will be either a trust corporation or at least 2 individuals to act as trustees to perform the trust; and

(d) any assurance or thing requisite for vesting the trust property, or any part thereof, in a sole trustee, or jointly in the persons who are the trustees, shall be executed or done.

(2) Nothing in this Ordinance shall authorize the appointment of a sole trustee, not being a trust corporation, where the trustee, when appointed, would be under the age of 21 years or would not be able to give valid receipts for all capital money arising under the trust.

Evidence as to a vacancy in a trust

39.(1) A statement, contained in any instrument coming into operation after the commencement of this Ordinance by which a new trustee is appointed for any purpose connected with land, to the effect that a trustee has remained out of Hong Kong for more than 12 months or refuses or is unfit to act, or is incapable of acting, or that he is not entitled to a beneficial interest in the trust property in possession, shall, in favour of a purchaser of a legal estate, be conclusive evidence of the matter stated.

(2) In favour of such purchaser any appointment of a new trustee depending on that statement, and any vesting declaration, express or implied, consequent on the appointment, shall be valid.

Retirement of trustee without a new appointment

40.(1) Where a trustee is desirous of being discharged from the trust, and after his discharge there will be either a trust corporation or at least 2 individuals to act as trustees to perform the trust, then, if such trustee as aforesaid by deed declares that he is desirous of being discharged from the trust, and if his co-trustees and such other person, if any, as is empowered to appoint trustees, by deed consent to the discharge of the trustee, and to the vesting in the co-trustees alone of the trust property, the trustee desirous of being discharged shall be deemed to have retired from the trust, and shall, by the deed, be discharged therefrom under this Ordinance, without any new trustee being appointed in his place.

(2) Any assurance or thing requisite for vesting the trust property in the continuing trustees alone shall be executed or done.

Vesting of trust property in new or continuing trustees

41.(1) Where by a deed a new trustee is appointed to perform any trust, then-

> *(a)* if the deed contains a declaration by the appointor to the effect that any estate or interest in any land subject to the trust, or in any chattel so subject, or the right to recover or receive any debt or other thing in action so subject, shall vest in the persons who by virtue of the deed become or are the trustees for performing the trust, the deed shall operate, without any conveyance or assignment, to vest in those persons as joint tenants and for the purposes of the trust the estate, interest or right to which the declaration relates; and

> *(b)* if the deed is made after the commencement of this Ordinance and does not contain such a declaration, the deed shall, subject to any express provision to the contrary therein contained, operate as if it had contained such a declaration by the appointor

extending to all the estates, interests and rights with respect to which a declaration could have been made.

(2) Where by a deed a retiring trustee is discharged under the statutory power without a new trustee being appointed, then-

(a) if the deed contains such a declaration as aforesaid by the retiring and continuing trustees, and by the other person, if any, empowered to appoint trustees, the deed shall, without any conveyance or assignment, operate to vest in the continuing trustees alone, as joint tenants, and for the purposes of the trust, the estate, interest or right to which the declaration relates; and

(b) if the deed is made after the commencement of this Ordinance and does not contain such a declaration, the deed shall, subject to any express provision to the contrary therein contained, operate as if it had contained such a declaration by such person as aforesaid extending to all the estates, interests and rights with respect to which a declaration could have been made.

(3) An express vesting declaration, whether made before or after the commencement of this Ordinance, shall, notwithstanding that the estate, interest or right to be vested is not expressly referred to, and provided that the other statutory requirements were or are complied with, operate and be deemed always to have operated (but without prejudice to any express provision to the contrary contained in the deed of appointment or discharge) to vest in the persons respectively referred to in subsections (1) and (2), as the case may require, such estates, interests and rights as are capable of being and ought to be vested in those persons.

(4) This section does not extend-

(a) to land conveyed by way of mortgage for securing money subject to the trust, except land conveyed on trust for securing debentures or debenture stock;

(b) to land held under a lease which contains any covenant, condition or agreement against assignment or disposing of the land without licence or consent, unless, prior to the execution of the deed containing expressly or impliedly the vesting declaration, the requisite licence or consent has been obtained, or unless, by virtue of any statute or rule of law, the vesting declaration, express or implied, would not operate as a breach of covenant or give rise to a forfeiture;

(c) to any share, stock, annuity or property which is only

transferable in books kept by a company or other body, or in manner directed by or under any enactment.

In this subsection "lease" includes an underlease and an agreement for a lease or underlease.

(5) For purposes of registration of the deed, the person or persons making the declaration, expressly or impliedly, shall be deemed the conveying party or parties, and the conveyance shall be deemed to be made by him or them under a power conferred by this Ordinance.

(6) This section applies to deeds of appointment or discharge executed on or after 1 July 1901.

PART V - Powers of The Court

Appointment of new Trustees

Power of court to appoint new trustees

42.(1) The court may, whenever it is expedient to appoint a new trustee or new trustees, and it is found inexpedient, difficult or impracticable so to do without the assistance of the court, make an order appointing a new trustee or new trustees either in substitution for or in addition to any existing trustee or trustees, or although there is no existing trustee. In particular and without prejudice to the generality of the foregoing provision, the court may make an order appointing a new trustee in substitution for a trustee who is sentenced to a term of imprisonment or is a lunatic or a person of unsound mind or is a bankrupt or is a corporation which is in liquidation or has been dissolved.

(2) An order under this section, and any consequential vesting order or conveyance, shall not operate further or otherwise as a discharge to any former or continuing trustee than an appointment of new trustees under any power for that purpose contained in any instrument would have operated.

(3) Nothing in this section gives power to appoint an executor or administrator.

Power to authorize remuneration

43. Where the court appoints a corporation, other than the Public Trustee in England, to be a trustee either solely or jointly with another person, the court may authorize the corporation to charge such remuneration for its services as trustee as the court may think fit.

Powers of new trustee appointed by court

44. Every trustee appointed by a court of competent jurisdiction shall, as well before as after the trust property becomes by law, or by assurance, or otherwise, vested in him, have the same powers, authorities, and discretions, and may in all respects act as if he had been originally appointed a trustee by the instrument, if any, creating the trust.

Vesting Orders

Vesting orders of land

45. In any of the following cases, namely-

> *(a)* where the court appoints or has appointed a trustee, or where a trustee has been appointed out of court under any statutory or express power;

> *(b)* where a trustee entitled to or possessed of any land or interest therein, whether by way of mortgage or otherwise, or entitled to

a contingent right therein, either solely or jointly with any other person -

    (i)   is under disability; or

    (ii)   is out of the jurisdiction of the court; or

    (iii)   cannot be found, or, being a corporation, has been dissolved;

(c)   where it is uncertain who was the survivor of 2 or more trustees jointly entitled to or possessed of any interest in land;

(d)   where it is uncertain whether the last trustee known to have been entitled to or possessed of any interest in land is living or dead;

(e)   where there is no personal representative of a deceased trustee who was entitled to or possessed of any interest in land, or where it is uncertain who is the personal representative of a deceased trustee who was entitled to or possessed of any interest in land;

(f)   where a trustee jointly or solely entitled to or possessed of any interest in land, or entitled to a contingent right therein, has been required, by or on behalf of a person entitled to require a conveyance of the land or interest or a release of the right, to convey the land or interest or to release the right, and has wilfully refused or neglected to convey the land or interest or release the right for 28 days after the date of the requirement;

(g)   where land or any interest therein is vested in a trustee whether by way of mortgage or otherwise, and it appears to the court to be expedient,

the court may make an order (in this Ordinance called a vesting order) vesting the land or interest therein in any such person in any such manner and for any such estate or interest as the court may direct, or releasing or disposing of the contingent right to such person as the court may direct:

Provided that-

    (i)   where the order is consequential on the appointment of a trustee the land or interest therein shall be vested for such estate as the court may direct in the persons who on the appointment are the trustees; and

(ii)   where the order relates to a trustee entitled or formerly entitled jointly with another person, and such trustee is under disability or out of the jurisdiction of the court or cannot be found, or being a corporation has been dissolved, the land, interest or right shall be vested in such other person who remains entitled, either alone or with any other person the court may appoint.

Orders as to contingent rights of unborn persons

46. Where any interest in land is subject to a contingent right in an unborn person or class of unborn persons who, on coming into existence would, in respect thereof, become entitled to or possessed of that interest on any trust, the court may make an order releasing the land or interest therein from the contingent right, or may make an order vesting in any person the estate or interest to or of which the unborn person or class of unborn persons would, on coming into existence, be entitled or possessed in the land.

Vesting order in place of conveyance by infant mortgagee

47. Where any person entitled to or possessed of any interest in land, or entitled to a contingent right in land, by way of security for money, is an infant, the court may make an order vesting or releasing or disposing of the interest in the land or the right in like manner as in the case of a trustee under disability.

Vesting order consequential on order for sale or mortgage of land

48. Where any court gives a judgment or makes an order directing the sale or mortgage of any land, every person who is entitled to or possessed of any interest in the land, or entitled to a contingent right therein, and is a party to the action or proceeding in which the judgment or order is given or made or is otherwise bound by the judgment or order, shall be deemed to be so entitled or possessed, as the case may be, as a trustee for the purposes of this Ordinance, and the court may, if it thinks expedient, make an order vesting the land or any part thereof for such estate or interest as the court thinks fit in the purchaser or mortgagee or in any other person.

Vesting order consequential on judgment for specific performance, etc.

49. Where a judgment is given for the specific performance of a contract concerning any interest in land, or for sale or exchange of any interest in land, or generally where any judgment is given for the conveyance of any interest in land either in cases arising out of the doctrine of election or otherwise, the court may declare-

>   *(a)*   that any of the parties to the action are trustees of any interest in the land or any part thereof within the meaning of this Ordinance; or

(b)   that the interests of unborn persons who might claim under any party to the action, or under the will or voluntary settlement of any deceased person who was during his lifetime a party to the contract or transaction concerning which the judgment is given, are the interests of persons who, on coming into existence, would be trustees within the meaning of this Ordinance,

and thereupon the court may make a vesting order relating to the rights of those persons, born and unborn, as if they had been trustees.

Effect of vesting order

50. A vesting order under any of the foregoing provisions shall in the case of a vesting order consequential on the appointment of a trustee, have the same effect-

(a)   as if the persons who before the appointment were the trustees, if any, had duly executed all proper conveyances of the land for such estate or interest as the court directs; or

(b)   if there is no such person, or no such person of full capacity, as if such person had existed and been of full capacity and had duly executed all proper conveyances of the land for such estate or interest as the court directs,

and shall in every other case have the same effect as if the trustee, or other person or description or class of persons to whose rights or supposed rights the said provisions respectively relate had been an ascertained and existing person of full capacity, and had executed a conveyance or release to the effect intended by the order.

Power to appoint person to convey

51. In all cases where a vesting order can be made under any of the foregoing provisions, the court may, if it is more convenient, appoint a person to convey the land or any interest therein or release the contingent right, and a conveyance or release by that person in conformity with the order shall have the same effect as an order under the appropriate provision.

Vesting orders as to stock and thing in action

52.(1) In any of the following cases, namely-

(a)   where the court appoints or has appointed a trustee, or where a trustee has been appointed out of court under any statutory or express power;

(b)   where a trustee entitled, whether by way of mortgage or otherwise, alone or jointly with another person to stock or to a thing in action-

(i) is under disability; or

(ii) is out of the jurisdiction of the court; or

(iii) cannot be found, or, being a corporation, has been dissolved; or

(iv) neglects or refuses to transfer stock or receive the dividends or income thereof, or to sue for or recover a thing in action, according to the direction of the person absolutely entitled thereto for 28 days next after a request in writing has been made to him by the person so entitled; or

(v) neglects or refuses to transfer stock or receive the dividends or income thereof, or to sue for or recover a thing in action for 28 days next after an order of the court for that purpose has been served on him;

(c) where it is uncertain whether a trustee entitled alone or jointly with another person to stock or to a thing in action is alive or dead;

(d) where stock is standing in the name of a deceased person whose personal representative is under disability;

(e) where stock or a thing in action is vested in a trustee whether by way of mortgage or otherwise and it appears to the court to be expedient,

the court may make an order vesting the right to transfer or call for a transfer of stock, or to receive the dividends or income thereof, or to sue for or recover the thing in action, in any such person as the court may appoint:

Provided that-

(i) where the order is consequential on the appointment of a trustee, the right shall be vested in the persons who, on the appointment, are the trustees; and

(ii) where the person whose right is dealt with by the order was entitled jointly with another person, the right shall be vested in that last-mentioned person either alone or jointly with any other person whom the court may appoint.

(2) In all cases where a vesting order can be made under this section, the court may, if it is more convenient, appoint some proper person to make or join in making the transfer:

Provided that the person appointed to make or join in making a transfer of stock shall be some proper officer of the bank, or the company or society whose stock is to be transferred.

(3) The person in whom the right to transfer or call for the transfer of any stock is vested by an order of the court under this Ordinance may transfer the stock to himself or any other person, according to the order, and all companies, banks and societies shall obey every order under this section according to its tenor.

(4) After notice in writing of an order under this section it shall not be lawful for any company, bank or society to transfer any stock to which the order relates or to pay any dividends thereon except in accordance with the order.

(5) The court may make declarations and give directions concerning the manner in which the right to transfer any stock or thing in action vested under the provisions of this Ordinance is to be exercised.

(6) The provisions of this Ordinance as to vesting orders shall apply to shares in ships registered under the enactments relating to merchant shipping as if they were stock.

Vesting orders of charity property

53. The powers conferred by this Ordinance as to vesting orders may be exercised for vesting any interest in land, stock or thing in action in any trustee of a charity or society over which the court would have jurisdiction upon action duly instituted, whether the appointment of the trustee was made by instrument under a power or by the court under its general or statutory jurisdiction.

Vesting orders in relation to infant's beneficial interest

54. Where an infant is beneficially entitled to any property, the court may, with a view to the application of the capital or income thereof for the maintenance, education or benefit of the infant, make an order-

> *(a)* appointing a person to convey such property; or

> *(b)* in the case of stock, or a thing in action, vesting in any person the right to transfer or call for a transfer of such stock, or to receive the dividends or income thereof, or to sue for and recover such thing in action, upon such terms as the court may think fit.

Orders made upon certain allegations
to be conclusive evidence

55. Where a vesting order is made as to any land under this Ordinance founded on an allegation of any of the following matters namely-

(a)   the personal incapacity of a trustee or mortgagee; or

(b)   that a trustee or mortgagee or the personal representative of or other person deriving title under a trustee or mortgagee is out of the jurisdiction of the court or cannot be found, or being a corporation has been dissolved; or

(c)   that it is uncertain which of 2 or more trustees, or which of 2 or more persons interested in a mortgage, was the survivor; or

(d)   that it is uncertain whether the last trustee or the personal representative of or other person deriving title under a trustee or mortgagee, or the last surviving person interested in a mortgage is living or dead; or

(e)   that any trustee or mortgagee has died intestate without leaving a person beneficially interested under the intestacy or has died and it is not known who is his personal representative or the person interested,

the fact that the order has been so made shall be conclusive evidence of the matter so alleged in any court upon any question as to the validity of the order; but this section does not prevent the court from directing a reconveyance or surrender or the payment of costs occasioned by any such order if improperly obtained.

Jurisdiction to make other Order.
Power of court to authorize dealing with trust property

56.(1) Where in the management or administration of any property vested in trustees, any sale, lease, mortgage, surrender, release, or other disposition, or any purchase, investment, acquisition, expenditure, or other transaction, is in the opinion of the court expedient, but the same cannot be effected by reason of the absence of any power for that purpose vested in the trustees by the trust instrument, if any, or by law, the court may by order confer upon the trustees, either generally or in any particular instance, the necessary power for the purpose, on such terms, and subject to such provisions and conditions, if any, as the court may think fit and may direct in what manner any money authorized to be expended, and the costs of any transaction, are to be paid or borne as between capital and income.

(2) The court may, from time to time, rescind or vary any order under this section, or may make any new or further order.

(3) An application to the court under this section may be made by the trustees, or by any of them, or by any person beneficially interested under the trust.

Persons entitled to apply for orders

57.(1) An order under this Ordinance for the appointment of a new trustee or concerning any interest in land, stock, or thing in action subject to a trust, may be made on the application of any person beneficially interested in the land, stock, or thing in action, whether under disability or not, or on the application of any person duly appointed trustee thereof.

(2) An order under this Ordinance concerning any interest in land, stock, or thing in action subject to a mortgage may be made on the application of any person beneficially interested in the equity of redemption, whether under disability or not, or of any person interested in the money secured by the mortgage.

Power to give judgment in absence of a trustee

58. Where in any action the court is satisfied that diligent search has been made for any person who, in the character of trustee, is made a defendant in any action, to serve him with a process of the court, and that he cannot be found, the court may hear and determine the action and give judgment therein against that person in his character of a trustee as if he had been duly served, or had entered an appearance in the action, and had also appeared by his solicitor at the hearing, but without prejudice to any interest he may have in the matters in question in the action in any other character.

Power to charge costs on trust estate

59. The court may order the costs and expenses of and incident to any application for an order appointing a new trustee, or for a Vesting order, or of and incident to any such order, or any conveyance or transfer in pursuance thereof, to be raised and paid out of the property in respect whereof the same is made, or out of the income thereof, or to be borne and paid in such manner and by such persons as to the court may seem just.

Power to relieve trustee from personal liability

60. If it appears to the court that a trustee, whether appointed by the court or otherwise, is or may be personally liable for any breach of trust, whether the transaction alleged to be a breach of trust occurred before or after the commencement of this Ordinance, but has acted honestly and reasonably, and ought fairly to be excused for the breach of trust and for omitting to obtain the directions of the court in the matter in which he committed such breach, then the court may relieve him either wholly or partly from personal liability for the same.

Power to make beneficiary indemnify for breach of trust

61.(1) Where a trustee commits a breach of trust at the instigation or request or with the consent in writing of a beneficiary, the court may, if it thinks fit, make such order as to the court seems just, for impounding all or any part of the interest of the beneficiary in the trust estate by way of indemnity to the trustee or persons claiming through him.

(2) This section applies to breaches of trust committed as well before as after the commencement of this Ordinance.

Payment into Court
Payment into court by trustees

62.(1) Trustees, or the majority of trustees, having in their hands or under their control money or securities belonging to a trust, may pay the same into court, and the same shall, subject to the rules of court, be dealt with according to the orders of the court.

(2) The receipt or certificate of the proper officer shall be a sufficient discharge to trustees for the money or securities so paid into court.

(3) Where money or securities is or are vested in any persons as trustees, and the majority are desirous of paying the same into court, but the concurrence of the other or others cannot be obtained, the court may order the payment into court to be made by the majority without the concurrence of the other or others.

(4) Where any such money or securities is or are deposited with any banker, broker, or other depositary, the court may order payment or delivery of the money or securities to the majority of the trustees for the purpose of payment into court.

(5) Every transfer, payment and delivery made in pursuance of any such order shall be valid and take effect as if the same had been made on the authority or by the act of all the persons entitled to the money and securities so transferred, paid or delivered.

PART VI - The Judicial Trustee

Power of court on application to appoint judicial trustee

63.(1) Where application is made to the court by or on behalf of the person creating or intending to create a trust, or by or on behalf of a trustee or beneficiary, or by the Attorney General in the case of a charitable trust, the court may, in its discretion, appoint a person (in this Part called a judicial trustee) to be a trustee of that trust, either jointly with any other person or as sole trustee, and, if sufficient cause is shown, in place of all or any existing trustees.

(2) The administration of the property of a deceased person, whether a testator or intestate, shall be a trust, and the executor or administrator a trustee, within the meaning of this Part.

(3) Any fit and proper person nominated for the purpose in the application may be appointed a judicial trustee, and, in the absence of such nomination, or if the court is not satisfied of the fitness of a person so nominated, an official of the court may be appointed, and in any case a judicial trustee shall be subject to the control and supervision of the court as an officer thereof.

(4) The court may, either on request or without request, give to a judicial trustee any general or special directions in regard to the trust or the administration thereof.

(5) There may be paid to the judicial trustee out of the trust property such remuneration, not exceeding any prescribed limits, as the court may assign in each case, subject to any rules under this Part respecting the application of such remuneration where the judicial trustee is an official of the court, and the remuneration so assigned to any judicial trustee shall, save as the court may for special reasons otherwise order, cover all his work and personal outlay.

(6) Once in every year the accounts of every trust of which a judicial trustee has been appointed shall be audited, and a report thereon made to the court by such persons as may be prescribed, and, in any case where the court shall so direct, an inquiry into the administration by a judicial trustee of any trust, or into any dealing or transaction of a judicial trustee, shall be made in such manner as may be prescribed.

Rules

64. The Chief Justice may with the approval of the Legislative Council make rules for carrying into effect this Part of this Ordinance and especially to prescribe or provide for-

> *(a)* requiring judicial trustees, who are not officials of the court, to give security for the due application of any trust property under their control;

> *(b)* the safety of the trust property, and the custody thereof;

> *(c)* the remuneration of judicial trustees and the fees to be taken

under this Part so as to cover the expenses of the administration of this Part, and the payment of such remuneration and fees out of the trust property, and, where the judicial trustee is an official of the court, the application of the remuneration and fees payable to him;

(d) dispensing with formal proof of facts in proper cases;

(e) facilitating the discharge by the court of administrative duties under this Part without judicial proceedings and otherwise regulating procedure under this Part and making it simple and inexpensive;

(f) the suspension or removal of any judicial trustee, and the succession of another person to the office of any judicial trustee who may cease to hold office, and the vesting in such person of any trust property;

(g) the classes of trusts in which officials of the court are not to be judicial trustees, or are to be so temporarily or conditionally;

(h) the procedure to be followed where the judicial trustee is executor or administrator;

(i) preventing the employment by judicial trustees of other persons at the expense of the trust, except in cases of strict necessity;

(j) filing and auditing of the accounts of any trust of which a judicial trustee has been appointed.

Definitions

65. In this Part-

"official of the court" means-

(a) the Official Solicitor; or

(b) the holder of such paid office in or connected with the court as may be prescribed;

"prescribed" means prescribed by rules made under this Part.

PART VII - The Official Trustee

Appointment of Official Trustee

66.(1) For the purpose of carrying into effect the provisions of this Part, it shall be lawful for the Governor to appoint a fit and proper person to be Official Trustee:

Provided that, until such appointment is made, the Official Solicitor shall ex officio exercise all the powers, privileges and discretions, and discharge the duties required to be performed by the Official Trustee under this Ordinance.

(2) The said office shall have perpetual succession, and all lands or any interest therein, and all moneys, stocks, and securities and land which may be vested in the Official Trustee under this Part shall be deemed to be vested in the Official Trustee for the time being, without any further transfer or conveyance.

Payment of trust moneys into bank to credit of Official Trustee

67.(1) Trustees, or the majority of trustees, having in their hands or under their control any moneys belonging to any trust, shall be at liberty, on filing in the Registry of the court an affidavit shortly describing the instrument creating the trust, according to the best of their knowledge and belief, to pay the same, with the consent of the Official Trustee and in accordance with such directions as they may receive for the purpose from him, into the court; and the said trust moneys shall be paid through the Treasury into a bank authorized by the Governor on deposit bearing interest, or otherwise, to the account of the Official Trustee (by his official designation) in the matter of the particular trust (describing the same by the names of the parties, as accurately as may be, for the purpose of distinguishing it), in trust to attend the orders of the court.

(2) Any trust moneys paid into a bank pursuant to subsection (1) which-

    (a)   remain unclaimed for a period of 5 years from the last making of any order of the Court in relation thereto; or

    (b)   if no such order shall have been made, remain unclaimed for a period of 5 years from the date of payment into the bank,

shall be transferred by the Official Trustee to the general revenue of Hong Kong.

Transfer of trust securities into name of Official Trustee

68. Trustees, or the majority of trustees, having any securities standing in their names in the books of any public company or corporation established in Hong Kong, or in the names of any deceased persons of whom they are personal representatives, upon any trust, shall be at liberty, on filing such affidavit as aforesaid, to transfer such securities, with such consent and in accordance with such directions as aforesaid, into the name of the Official Trustee (by his official designation) or to deposit the same in his name in such bank as aforesaid in the matter of the particular trust (describing the same as aforesaid), in trust to attend the orders of the court.

Conveyance of land in trust to Official Trustee

69. Trustees, or the majority of trustees, in whom any land within Hong Kong is or becomes vested upon any trust, shall be at liberty, on filing such affidavit as aforesaid, to convey such land, with such consent and in accordance with such directions as aforesaid, to the Official Trustee, in trust to attend the orders of the court.

Certificate to be given by Official Trustee

70. In every such case as aforesaid, the certificate of the Official Trustee for the moneys so paid, or of the transfer or deposit of such securities, or of the conveyance of such land shall be a sufficient discharge to such trustees for the moneys so paid, or the stocks or securities so transferred or deposited, or the land so conveyed as aforesaid.

Order for payment, etc. by majority of trustees

without concurrence of others

71.(1) Where any moneys or securities, or any land, are or is vested in any persons as trustees, and the majority of them are desirous of paying, transferring, depositing, or conveying the same as aforesaid, but the concurrence of the other or others cannot be obtained, the court may order the payment, transfer, deposit, or conveyance to be made by the majority without the concurrence of the other or others; and where any such moneys or securities are deposited with any banker, broker, or other depositary, the court may order payment or delivery of the moneys or securities to the majority of the trustees for the purpose of payment into court.

(2) Every payment, transfer, deposit, delivery, and conveyance made in pursuance of any such order shall be valid and take effect as if the same had been made on the authority or by the act of all the persons entitled to the moneys, securities, or land so paid, transferred, deposited, delivered, or conveyed.

Administration of trust estate

72.(1) Such orders as may seem fit shall be made by the court in respect of the trust estate and for the investment and payment of any such moneys or of any dividends or interest on any such securities, and for the transfer and delivery out of any such securities, and for the administration of any such trust generally, upon a petition to be presented in a summary way to the court by such party or parties as to the court may appear to be competent and necessary in that behalf, and service of such petition shall be made on such person or persons as the court may see fit and direct.

(2) Every order made upon any such petition shall have the same authority and effect, and shall be enforced in the same manner, as if the same had been made in an action regularly instituted in the court.

(3) If in any case it appears that the trust estate cannot be safely administered without the institution of one or more action or actions, the court may direct any such action or actions to be instituted.

Charges upon trust estate administered by Official Trustee

73.(1) There shall be imposed and levied, for the use of the Crown, upon every trust estate administered under this Part a charge equivalent to the following percentage of the net value of the trust estate -10 per cent where the value of the trust estate does not exceed $100,000, or, where the value exceeds $100,000, 10 per cent on the first $ 100,000 and 5 per cent on the excess.

(2) The said charge shall constitute a primary lien upon the trust estate, and shall be levied, in the case of trust moneys deposited in a bank, by an order of the court, authorizing the payment thereof to the Official Trustee for the use of the Crown, and in the case of securities or land, by sale, mortgage, or otherwise as the court may direct, and in case of any such sale or mortgage, the court may, by the same or any further order, empower the Official Trustee to execute all instruments necessary for carrying out this provision, and instruments so executed shall be as valid and effectual to all intents and purposes as if the same had been executed by all persons who, but for this provision, would have been necessary parties thereto.

(3) There shall also be imposed and levied, for the use of the Crown, upon every such estate a charge equivalent to 5 per cent of the annual revenue of the trust estate. The Official Trustee shall deduct such charge in making up the annual accounts of the estate.

General rights and powers of Official Trustee

74.(1) In the administration of any trust estate, the Official Trustee shall have and may exercise all the rights and powers conferred upon trustees by this Ordinance, so far as they are applicable to such trust estate.

(2) The Official Trustee may, subject to any rules that may be made under section 76, employ for the purposes of any trust such solicitors, bankers, accountants, brokers or other persons, as he may consider necessary, and, in determining the persons to be employed in relation to any trust, he shall have regard to the interests of the trust, but subject to this he shall, whenever practicable, take into consideration the wishes of the creator of the trust and of the other trustees (if any) and of the beneficiaries, either expressed or implied by the practice of the creator of the trust, or in the previous management of the trust.

Limitation of liability of Official Trustee

75. The Official Trustee shall incur no personal liability by reason of any securities being transferred into his name as aforesaid, or by reason of any land being conveyed to him as aforesaid, or by reason of any loss accruing to any trust estate in his hands, otherwise than by his own wilful neglect or default:

Provided that nothing in this Part shall be deemed to affect any rights or remedies against the trust estate or any cestui que trust or any person other than the Official Trustee and the trustees so discharged as aforesaid.

Rules for administration of trust funds

76. The Governor in Council may make rules providing for the administration of trust funds.

PART VIII - Trust Companies

Application by company to be registered as a trust company

77.(1) Any company incorporated in Hong Kong (not being a private company within the meaning of section 29 of the Companies Ordinance (Cap. 32)) may apply in writing to the Registrar of Companies to be registered as a trust company under this Part.

(2) A company which makes an application under subsection (1) shall be eligible to be registered under this Part if, but only if-

- *(a)* the objects of the company as set out in its memorandum and articles of association are restricted to some or all of the objects set out in section 81;

- *(b)* the issued share capital of the company is not less than $3,000,000;

- *(c)* in the case of a company having an issued share capital of $3,000,000 that capital is bona fide fully paid up for a cash consideration and, in the case of a company having an issued share capital exceeding $3,000,000 at least $3,000,000 of that capital is bona fide paid up for a cash consideration;

- *(d)* the board of directors has been duly appointed in accordance with the articles of association of the company;

- *(e)* the company has either-

    - **(i)** deposited with the Director of Accounting Services investments specified in the Second Schedule (other than those specified in paragraphs 7, 14, 15, 17 and 19) to the value of not less than $1,500,000; or

    - **(ii)** deposited in the name of the Director of Accounting Services with a finance company that is a subsidiary of a bank within the meaning of section 2 of the Banking Ordinance (Cap.155) a sum not less than $1,500,000 and lodged a receipt issued by the finance company for that amount with the Director of Accounting Services; or

    - **(iii)** deposited with the Director of Accounting Services a guarantee, in terms acceptable to the Director of

Accounting Services, from a bank within the meaning of section 2 of the Banking Ordinance (Cap. 155); and

(f) the company is able to meet its obligations, apart from its liability to its shareholders, without taking into account the investments or sum deposited under paragraph (e).

(3) For the purposes of subsection (2) -

(a) "finance company" means a company whose principal business involves the receiving on deposit of money, whether repayable to depositors with or without interest or other consideration, and the lending of that money, or a substantial part of that money, to borrowers on terms that the money is repayable to the company or its nominee with interest or at a premium or with consideration in money or money's worth, but does not include a bank within the meaning of section 2 of the Banking Ordinance (Cap.155);

(b) section 2(4), (5) and (6) of the Companies Ordinance (Cap. 32) shall apply as if each reference in those subsections to "a company" or "first-mentioned company" were read as a reference to a finance company and as if each reference in those subsections to "another company" or "other company" were read as a reference to a bank within the meaning of section 2 of the Banking Ordinance (Cap. 155).

(4) A trust company registered under this Ordinance before the date of commencement of the Trustee (Amendment) Ordinance 1975 which has not previously complied with the requirements as to eligibility for registration as a trust company as set out in subsection (2) of this section shall, within 9 months after that date, comply with those requirements to the satisfaction of the Registrar of Companies.

(4A) Subject to subsection (4B), a trust company registered under this Ordinance, whether before, on or after the date of commencement of the Trustee (Amendment) Ordinance 1993, shall after its registration and for so long as it carries on any business or executes any office included in the objects set out in section 81(1) comply with the requirements set out in subsection (2).

(4B) A trust company registered before the date of commencement of the Trustee (Amendment) Ordinance 1993 which at that date does not comply with one or more of the requirements set out in subsection (2) shall, within 9 months after that date, comply with those requirements to the satisfaction of the Registrar of Companies.

(5) Notwithstanding section 7 of the Companies Ordinance (Cap. 32), a trust company to which subsection (4) or (4B) applies may, within the period of 9 months referred to in that subsection, alter any condition contained in its memorandum of association to such extent as may be required to enable it to comply with the requirements of subsection (2).

Issue of certificate

78.(1) On the receipt of an application under section 77, the Registrar of Companies shall make such inquiry as he deems necessary, and, if satisfied that all the requirements of section 77 have been complied with, shall register the company applying for registration as a trust company in the register prescribed by section 79 and shall issue to it a certificate that the company is registered as a trust company, and thereupon the company shall be invested with all the powers, privileges and immunities and shall be subject to all the liabilities imposed by this Part.

(2) Notice of the issue of such certificate shall be published by the Registrar of Companies in the Gazette for 4 consecutive weeks next following the issue.

(3) If the Registrar of Companies is not satisfied that all the requirements of section 77 have been complied with, he shall refuse to register the company as a trust company:

Provided that the company may appeal from such refusal to the Governor in Council, whose decision shall be final.

Register of trust companies to be kept

79. There shall be kept in the office of the Registrar of Companies a register, to be called the "Register of Trust Companies", in which shall be entered the names of all trust companies registered under this Ordinance, together with such other particulars as the Registrar of Companies may think necessary.

Deposit to be held as security

80.(1) From the time of the issue to any company of a certificate under section 78 the investments or the sum of money deposited under section 77 shall be held as security for the depositors and creditors of the company and for the faithful execution of all trusts which may be accepted by or imposed upon the company and for its obligations generally.

(2) If at any time, by reason of the decline in value of any investments so held by the Director of Accounting Services or of increase of the gross liabilities of any trust company, the Registrar of Companies is of opinion that additional security ought to be furnished by the trust company, he may order the company to make, within a period to be stated in the order, a further deposit of investments (being investments contemplated by section 77(2)(e)) of a specified value with the Director of Accounting Services:

Provided that the company may appeal from such order to the Governor in Council, whose decision shall be final.

(3) A trust company may, with the approval of the Director of Accounting Services and subject to such terms as he may specify-

    (a)   substitute-

        (i)   other investments contemplated by sub-paragraph (i) of paragraph (e) of section 77(2) for all or any of the investments deposited with the Director of Accounting Services under that sub-paragraph; or

        (ii)   a sum of money, as contemplated by sub-paragraph (ii) of that paragraph, for the investments so deposited; or

    (b)   if the company has deposited a sum of money under sub-paragraph (ii) of paragraph (e) of section 77(2), withdraw the sum and either-

        (i)   deposit it with another finance company; or

        (ii)   substitute for the sum of money so withdrawn investments contemplated by sub-paragraph (i) of that paragraph.

(4) All money accruing by way of dividends or interest in respect of investments deposited with the Director of Accounting Services or in respect of sums deposited with a finance company under this Part shall be paid to the trust company which made the deposit.

Objects

81.(1) The objects of a trust company may be some or all of, but shall not exceed the following-

    (a)   to accept and execute the offices of executor, administrator, trustee, receiver, receiver and manager, assignee, liquidator, guardian of the property of infants, committee of the estates of lunatics, or other like office of a fiduciary nature;

    (b)   to act as attorney or agent for the collection, receipt and payment of money and for winding up estates and for the sale or purchase of any movable or immovable property;

    (c)   to act as agent for the management and control of movable and immovable property for and on behalf of the owners thereof or for or on behalf of executors, administrators or trustees;

(d)   to act as investing and financial agent for and on behalf of executors, administrators, and trustees or any other persons whatsoever and to receive money in trust for investment and to allow interest thereon until invested; and to undertake for and on behalf of executors, administrators and trustees or any other persons whatsoever the negotiation of loans of all descriptions and the procuring and lending of money on the security of any description of property immovable or movable or without taking any security on such terms as may be arranged, and to advance and lend moneys to protect any estate, trust or property entrusted to the company as aforesaid and to charge interest upon any such advances:

Provided that nothing herein contained shall be held either to restrict or extend the powers of the company as trustee or agent under the terms of any trust or agency that may be conferred upon it;

(e)   to take securities of such nature as are deemed expedient for any moneys owing to the company;

(f)   to be the custodian on such terms as are agreed upon of any moneys, securities, jewellery, plate or other valuable property and of papers, documents, deeds, wills, debentures and other evidence of title or indebtedness;

(g)   to receive and manage any sinking, redemption, guarantee or any other special fund or deposit and to act as agent for countersigning, registering or otherwise ascertaining and certifying to the genuineness of any issue of shares, stocks, bonds, debentures or other securities for money of any government, municipal or other corporate body or of any association, whether incorporated or not, duly authorized to issue and make such issue and to hold any such securities as agent or trustee and to act generally as agent for any such government, municipal or corporate body or association;

(h)   to acquire and hold immovable property for the actual use and occupation of the company or any of its officers and servants and to erect, construct, enlarge, alter and maintain any buildings necessary or convenient for the said purposes and to sell or otherwise dispose of any such immovable property if not required for the said purposes;

(i)   to hold land which having been mortgaged to the company is

acquired by it for the protection of its investments; and from time to time sell, mortgage, lease or otherwise dispose thereof;

(j) to deposit the moneys of the company not immediately required with any bank or banks at interest until such moneys can be more permanently invested and to invest the moneys of the company in accordance with the provisions of section 91;

(k) to borrow moneys and secure the repayment thereof with interest in accordance with the provisions of section 93;

(l) to receive and collect such remuneration for its services as is agreed upon or as fixed or allowed from time to time by law and all usual and customary charges, costs and expenses;

(m) to support and subscribe to any charitable or public object and any institution, society or club which may be for the benefit of the company or its employees or may be connected with any town or place where the company carries on business; to give pensions, gratuities or charitable aid to any person or persons who may serve or have served the company or to the wives, children or other relatives of such persons; to make payments towards insurance and to form and contribute to provident and benefit funds for the benefit of any persons employed by the company:

Provided that no such subscription, gift, payment or contribution shall be given or made, except out of profits of the company available for distribution as dividend;

(n) to acquire and undertake the whole or any part of the business of any person or company of a like nature to any business which a trust company is authorized to carry on and in consideration for such acquisition to undertake all or any of the liabilities of such person or company and to issue shares to such person or company;

(o) to do all such other things as are incidental or conductive to the attainment of the before-mentioned objects or any of them;

(p) to carry out all or any of the objects aforesaid either within or outside Hong Kong and by or through trustees, agents or otherwise and either alone or in conjunction with others.

(2) Nothing in this section shall be construed to authorize any trust company to engage in the business of banking or of insurance or the business of a deposit, provident or benefit society.

(3) No trust company shall carry on any business or execute any office other than the businesses or offices included in the objects set out in subsection (1).

(4) For the avoidance of doubt it is hereby declared that nothing in subsection (1) shall be construed so as to restrict, or at any time to have restricted, a trust company to carrying out its objects within Hong Kong only.

Trust company may act as executor

82. If at any time a trust company shall be appointed executor of the will of any testator, it shall be lawful for the company to apply to the court for probate of the will and if probate be granted, to exercise and discharge all the powers and duties of an executor.

Trust company to apply for probate or administration

83.(1) If and whenever any person shall be entitled to apply for probate of the will of any testator without leave being reserved to any other person to apply for probate, it shall be lawful for such person, whether absent from Hong Kong or not, and notwithstanding the provisions of any other enactment, instead of himself applying for such probate, to authorize a trust company to apply to the court for a grant of administration with the will annexed of the estate of such testator, and such grant may be made to the trust company upon its own application, when so authorized, but the provisions of this section shall not apply to any case in which a will provides that a company shall not act as executor or in the trusts thereof.

(2) If and whenever any person shall be entitled to apply for letters of administration with the will of any testator annexed of the estate of such testator, it shall be lawful for such person, whether absent from Hong Kong or not, and notwithstanding the provisions of any other enactment, to authorize a trust company, either alone, or jointly with any other person, to apply to the court for a grant of letters of administration with the will annexed of the estate of such testator, and such grant may be made to the company upon its own application when so authorized, but the provisions of this section shall not apply to a case in which a will provides that a company shall not act as executor, or in the trusts thereof.

(3) It shall be lawful for any person or persons entitled to apply for administration of the estate of any intestate, whether such person or persons be absent from Hong Kong or not, and notwithstanding the provisions of any other enactment, to authorize a trust company to apply to the court for such letters of administration, either alone or jointly with any other person, and administration of the estate of any such intestate may be granted to the company either alone or jointly as aforesaid, upon its own application, when so authorized.

(4) For the purposes of any application to the court for letters of administration to the estate of any deceased person, the court shall consider a trust company, when authorized as aforesaid, to be in law entitled, equally with any other person or class of persons to apply for and obtain a grant, but a trust company, being so entitled, shall not on that account alone, be preferred to the widower, widow, or next-of-kin of any intestate.

(5) No grant of probate or of letters of administration shall be granted to a syndic or nominee on behalf of a trust company.

(6) Where any person entitled to apply for probate or letters of administration has authorized a trust company to apply for a grant in favour of the company under subsection (1) or (2) and the court has subsequently made such a grant, all property, functions, powers, authorities, discretions and rights vested in or conferred on that person by the will or by law shall, on the making of the grant and without conveyance or assignment or the execution of any other instrument, become vested in and exercisable by the company as fully and effectually as if it had been named as executor under the will.

Procedure as to petitions, etc.

84.(1) In all cases in which a trust company is empowered under this Part to apply for probate or letters of administration, any petition, declaration, account or affidavit or other necessary document may be made or sworn by any officer of the company duly authorized by the company in that behalf.

(2) Any officer of the company appointed by a trust company for that purpose may, on behalf of the company, sign any petition, account or statement, take any oath, swear any affidavit, make any declaration, verify any act, give personal attendance at any court or place, and do any act or thing whatsoever, which may require to be signed, taken, sworn, made, verified, given, or done on behalf of the company:

Provided that nothing in this Part contained shall confer upon any person, not otherwise entitled thereto, any right to appear or be heard before or in any court on behalf of the company or to do any act whatsoever on behalf of the company which could otherwise be lawfully done only by a barrister or by a solicitor.

Appointment of a company to be a trustee

85. In all cases in which the court or any person or persons has or have power to appoint a trustee, whether as an original or new or additional trustee, to perform any legal trust or duty a trust company may be appointed in the same manner as if the company were a private individual:

Provided that-

> *(a)* no trust company shall be appointed in any case in which the instrument creating the trust, or the power authorizing the appointment, forbids the appointment of a company;

(b)   nothing in this section shall be deemed to derogate from the provisions of sections 38 and 40.

Joint tenancy

86. A trust company, acting in a fiduciary capacity, shall be capable of acquiring and holding any property in joint tenancy in the same manner as if it were a private individual.

Trust company may act as agent

87. It shall be lawful for a trust company to act under any deed or instrument by which the company is appointed agent or attorney for any person, and all the powers conferred upon the company by any such deed or instrument may be exercised by such officer of the company as the company may appoint for that purpose:

Provided that nothing in this section shall be deemed to authorize any person to confer upon a trust company any power which may not lawfully be delegated by him.

Security not required

88.(1) Notwithstanding the provisions of any other enactment, no trust company to which a grant of letters of administration has been made shall be required to furnish security for the due administration of the estate.

(2) Notwithstanding the provisions of any other enactment, no trust company appointed by the court to perform the duties of receiver, guardian, committee or any other office or trust shall be required to furnish security for the due performance of such duties.

Trust funds to be kept separate

89. All moneys, property and securities received or held by any trust company in a fiduciary capacity shall always be kept distinct from those of the company and in separate accounts, and so marked in the books of the company for each particular trust as always to be distinguished from any other in the registers and other books of account to be kept by the company, so that at no time shall trust moneys form part of or be mixed with the general assets of the company; and all investments made by the company as trustee shall be so designated that the trusts to which such investments belong can be readily identified at any time.

Investment of trust funds

90.(1) A trust company may invest trust moneys in its hands in or upon any securities in which private trustees may by law invest trust moneys and may from time to time vary any such investment for others of the same nature:

Provided that the company shall not in any case invest the moneys of any trust in or upon securities prohibited by the instrument creating the trust, and whenever any special directions are given in any order, judgment, decree or will or in any other instrument creating the trust, as to the particular class or kind of securities or property in or upon which any investment shall be made, the company shall follow such directions. The company may also, in its discretion, retain and continue any investment and securities coming into its possession in any fiduciary capacity.

(2) No trust company shall directly or indirectly invest any trust moneys otherwise than in accordance with the provisions of subsection (1).

Investment of trust company's own funds

91.(1) A trust company may invest moneys forming part of its own capital or reserve or accumulated profits-

> *(a)* in or upon any securities in or upon which private trustees may by law invest trust moneys; and

> *(b)* in or upon such other securities as the Financial Secretary may from time to time approve.

(2) A trust company may acquire and hold immovable property for the actual use and occupation of itself or of any of its officers or servants and may sell and dispose of the same.

(3) A trust company may, for the protection of its investments, acquire land which has been mortgaged to it, but shall sell any land so acquired within 3 years after the acquisition thereof, unless such time is extended by the Financial Secretary.

(4) No trust company shall directly or indirectly invest any of its moneys otherwise than in accordance with subsections (1), (2) and (3):

Provided that nothing in this section shall be deemed to prevent the acceptance by a trust company of any securities whatsoever to secure the payment of a debt previously contracted in good faith; but any security so acquired by the company which it would otherwise be prohibited from taking or holding shall, within 2 years from the time of its acquisition, or within such further time as may be allowed by the Registrar of Companies, be sold or disposed of.

Loans to trust company officers, etc. prohibited

92. No loan shall be made by any trust company to any director or other officer or servant thereof or to any company or firm in the management of which any such director or other officer or servant is actively engaged. If any loan is made in contravention of this section, all directors and officers of the company who made the loan or assented thereto shall be jointly and severally liable to the company for the amount thereof with interest.

Borrowing

93.(1) For the purpose of attaining the objects of the company as set out in section 81 (or such of them as the company may have adopted), and for no other purpose, a trust company may from time to time borrow money provided that the aggregate of the sums of money borrowed shall at no time exceed the amount of the company's capital for the time being paid up.

(2) Moneys borrowed by a trust company shall not be secured, by debenture or otherwise, on its capital or general undertaking, but may be secured on any of the company's property (not being property held by it on any trust), other than the securities deposited by it with the Director of Accounting Services under the provisions of this Part.

94. (*Repealed*)

Investigation by inspector

95.(1) The Financial Secretary may at any time appoint an inspector to investigate the affairs and management of any trust company if it appears to the Financial Secretary that there are circumstances suggesting-

    (a)   that the trust company has committed a breach of trust;

    (b)   that the business of the trust company has been or is being conducted with intent to defraud its creditors or the creditors of any other person or otherwise for a fraudulent or unlawful purpose or in a manner oppressive of any part of its members or that it was formed for any fraudulent or unlawful purpose;

    (c)   that persons concerned with its formation or the management of its affairs have in connection therewith been guilty of fraud, misfeasance or other misconduct towards it or towards its members;

    (d)   that its members have not been given all the information with respect to its affairs that they might reasonably expect;

    (e)   that it is insolvent; or

    (f)   that it has failed to comply with any of the requirements of this Part.

(1A) The Financial Secretary may give directions as to the manner in which and the extent to which an investigation under subsection (1) shall be conducted.

(2) It shall be the duty of all officers and servants of the company to produce for examination by the inspector all books, accounts, vouchers and other documents in their custody or control in relation to matters under investigation, and to answer truly all inquiries addressed to them by the inspector respecting any matter affecting the affairs of the company.

(3) The inspector shall make a report of his investigation to the Financial Secretary.

(4) All expenses of and incidental to any such investigation shall be paid by the company, if the Financial Secretary so directs.

Special provision as to winding up a trust company

96.(1) The court may order the winding up of a trust company in accordance with the Companies Ordinance (Cap. 32), and the provisions of that Ordinance shall apply accordingly subject however to the modification that the company may also be ordered to be wound up on application made by the Attorney General if-

(a) the company has made default in complying with a requirement of this Part and such default has continued for a period of 2 months after notice of default has been served upon the company; or

(b) from the consideration of the report of an inspector appointed under section 95 it appears that the company has committed a breach of trust.

(2) Upon the winding up of a trust company every person who has been a director of the company at any time within the period of 2 years immediately preceding the commencement of the winding up shall be liable for the balance unpaid on every share which he may have transferred during such 2 years.

Personal liability of officers of a trust company

97. Where a trust company holds the office of executor, administrator or trustee, every person employed by the company to discharge any of the duties of such office shall, in respect of the duties entrusted to him, be personally responsible to the court and be subject to the process of the court, as though he had been personally appointed to such office.

Offences

98.(1) Any director, officer or servant of a trust company who wilfully and with intent to defraud neglects to make any entry in the books of the company which it is his duty to make shall be guilty of an offence triable upon indictment.

(2) Any director, officer or servant of a trust company, who wilfully and with intent to defraud makes or abets the making of any false entry in the books of the company, or subscribes or exhibits any false document with intent to deceive any person appointed under this Part to investigate the affairs and management of the company shall be guilty of an offence triable upon indictment.

(3) Any director, officer or servant of a trust company who refuses to produce for examination to any person appointed under this Part to investigate the affairs and management of the company all books and documents relevant to such investigation which are in his custody or control shall be guilty of an offence triable upon indictment.

(4) A trust company which contravenes section 77(4), (4A) or (4B), 81(3), 91(4), 92 or 93 commits an offence and is liable on conviction to a fine of $25,000 and if the offence is continued after conviction the trust company commits a further offence and is liable on conviction to a fine of $1,000 for every day or part of a day on which the offence is so continued.

Not to be guardian or committee

99. No trust company shall be appointed to be guardian of the person of an infant or committee of the person of a lunatic.

Restriction on holding shares in trust company

100.(1) No member of a trust company shall at any time hold shares in the capital of the company to an amount exceeding one-fifth of the issued capital of the company for the time being.

(2) Subsection (1) does not apply to a trust company that is the subsidiary of a bank within the meaning of section 2 of the Banking Ordinance (Cap. 155).

(3) For the purposes of subsection (2) of this section, section 2(4), (5) and (6) of the Companies Ordinance (Cap. 32) shall apply as if each reference in those subsections to "a company" or "the first-mentioned company" were read as a reference to a trust company and as if each reference in those subsections to "another company" or "other company" were read as a reference to a bank within the meaning of section 2 of the Banking Ordinance (Cap. 155).

Voluntary winding-up or disposal may be restrained

101. So long as any estate in respect of which a trust company is trustee shall remain in whole or in part unadministered, it shall not be lawful to proceed to wind up the company voluntarily, unless with the sanction of the court, and it shall be lawful for any person interested in such estate, or who may have any claim in respect thereof, to apply to the court in a summary way by motion to restrain any director or any shareholder from disposing of any shares which such director or shareholder may hold in the company or to restrain the winding up voluntarily of the company; and the court shall have power to make such order as it deems just.

Liability and powers of trust company

102. Subject to the provisions of this Part, the liability of every trust company to the person or persons interested in any estate held by the company as executor, administrator, trustee, receiver, liquidator, assignee, guardian or committee or in any other official or business capacity shall be the same as if the estate had been held by a private person in the like capacity; and the powers of the company shall be the same as those of a private person in the like capacity.

Registration of a trust company as shareholder, etc. not notice of trust

103. Neither the application by a trust company for registration as a member or shareholder in the books of any company or corporation nor the entry of the name of a trust company in the books of any company or corporation shall constitute notice of trust, and no company or corporation shall be entitled to object to enter the name of a trust company on its books by reason only that the company may be or is a trustee, and, in dealings with property, the fact that the person or one of the persons dealt with is a trust company shall not of itself constitute notice of a trust.

Unclaimed money to be paid into court

104. All money and securities which shall remain in the hands of a trust company, as trustee, unclaimed by the person entitled to the same for a period of 6 years after the time when the same shall have become payable to such person (except where payment has been restrained by order of a court of competent jurisdiction), together with such interest, if any, as shall have been received by the company in respect thereof, less any commission or other charges properly chargeable by the company, shall be paid by the company into court under and in accordance with section 62:

Provided that it shall not be necessary for the company to comply with the provisions of this section more often than once in any year nor shall it be necessary for the company to obtain the concurrence or consent of any person to such payment into court.

Fees payable by trust companies

105.(1) There shall be paid by every trust company to the Registrar of Companies, in respect of the matters mentioned in the First Schedule, the several fees specified therein.

(2) All such fees shall be paid by the Registrar of Companies into the Treasury.

(3) It shall be lawful for the Governor from time to time, by notification in the Gazette, to add to or alter the First Schedule.

Registration of certain banking corporations as trust companies

106.(1) Notwithstanding the foregoing, any company lawfully carrying on banking business in Hong Kong and having a capital (in stock or shares) for the time being issued of not less than $4,000,000 (of which not less than $1,600,000 shall have been paid up in cash) may with the consent of the Governor be registered as a trust company:

Provided that the Governor shall not give such consent unless he is satisfied that the extent and nature of the company's business in Hong Kong is sufficient to justify such special registration.

(2) Consent of the Governor under subsection (1) shall be notified to the Registrar of Companies who shall register the company in the register prescribed by section 79, issue to it a certificate that the company is registered as a trust company, and publish notice thereof in the Gazette for 4 consecutive weeks next following such issue.

(3) The provisions of sections 77, 78, 80, 81, 91, 92, 93, 96 and 100 shall not apply to such company or to such registration, but subject to such exceptions and to the provisions of the succeeding section the said company shall be invested with all the powers, privileges and immunities and shall be subject to all the liabilities imposed by this Part.

Limitation of powers of inspectors under section 95

107. The powers of investigation conferred upon inspectors under section 95 shall in the case of a corporation registered as a trust company under section 106 be limited to the trust business of the corporation.

Striking off trust company registered under section 106

108. On application made by the Attorney General the court may order that any corporation registered under the provisions of section 106 as a trust company shall be struck off the register of trust companies if it ceases to be qualified for registration under that section or if from the consideration of the report of an inspector appointed under section 95 it appears that the corporation has committed a breach of trust, and the court may appoint a new trustee, or new trustees, for any trust property held by the corporation.

PART IX - General Provisions

Indemnity

109. This Ordinance, and every order purporting to be made under this Ordinance, shall be a complete indemnity to any bank and to all persons for any acts done pursuant thereto, and it shall not be necessary for any bank or person to inquire concerning the propriety of the order, or whether the court by which the order was made had jurisdiction to make it.

FIRST SCHEDULE

Fees To Be Paid By Trust Companies To The

Registrar Of Companies

1. On application for registration under section 77 .... $10,300

2. For certificate of registration under section 78-

       (a)   where the authorized capital does
            not exceed $500,000 ....$130

       (b)   where the authorized capital exceeds
            $500,000 but does not exceed $1,000,000..........................$385

       (c)   where the authorized capital exceeds $1,000,000 ....$770

SECOND SCHEDULE

Authorized Investments

1. Any shares or debentures which are issued or allotted by a company and which satisfy the following conditions at the date the investment is made

    (a)   in the case of shares-

        (i)   the shares are listed on the Unified Exchange or on a stock market specified in Schedule 2 to the Financial Resources Rules (Cap. 24 sub. leg.);

        (ii)   the market capitalization of the company issuing the shares is not less than $10 billion ($10,000,000,000) or its equivalent in foreign currency; and

        (iii)   the company has paid, in each of the 5 years immediately preceding the calendar year in which the investment is made, a dividend wholly in cash (except to the extent that any shareholder may have opted to accept it other than wholly in cash) on all the shares issued by the company, excluding any shares issued after the dividend was declared and any shares which by their terms of issue did not rank for the dividend in that year;

    (b)   In the case of debentures, the security meets the credit rating as specified in the Table.

For the purposes of subparagraph (a)(iii) a company formed-

        (i)   to take over the business of another company or other companies; or

        (ii)   to acquire the securities of, or control of, another company or other companies,

or for either of those purposes and for other purposes shall be deemed to have paid a dividend as mentioned in that subparagraph in any year in which such a dividend has been paid by the other company or all the other companies, as the case may be.

2. Any debt security which is issued by, or the payment of principal and interest on which is guaranteed by-

(a)   in Hong Kong, the Government of Hong Kong, the Exchange Fund established by the Exchange Fund Ordinance (Cap. 66) or a company 100% of the shares in which are owned beneficially by the Government of Hong Kong; or

(b)   outside Hong Kong, the government, the central bank or an equivalent agency of a country which qualifies for the credit rating specified in the Table; or

(c)   any multilateral agency specified in Part III of the Schedule to the Protection of Investors Ordinance (Cap. 335) which qualifies for the credit rating specified in the Table.

3.   Any mutual fund corporation or unit trust authorized under section 15 of the Securities Ordinance (Cap. 333) for the purposes of that Ordinance.

4.   Any deposit (as defined in section 2 of the Banking Ordinance (Cap. 155)) with an authorized institution.

5.   Certificates of deposit, bills of exchange, promissory notes or short-term i.e. less than 1 year) debt securities issued or guaranteed by an authorized institution or by an exempted body.

6.   First legal mortgages of any property, including an undivided share in property, which is situated in Hong Kong and held under a Crown lease of which the unexpired term at the time of investment is not less than 50 years, excluding any term for which the lease can be renewed.

7.   Any derivatives which are traded on a market listed in Schedule 5 to the Financial Resources Rules (Cap. 24 sub. leg.); except that an investment under this paragraph-

(a)   shall be made for hedging purposes only, that is to say, the derivatives acquired shall be of a type and specification suitable for reducing the impact on the trust fund of a diminution in the value of specific assets already held by the trust fund or which are to be acquired at the same time as the derivatives; and

(b)   shall not be made except in accordance with the written advice of an investment adviser (as defined in section 2 of the Securities Ordinance (Cap. 333)) or of a commodity trading adviser (as defined in section 2 of the Commodities Trading Ordinance (Cap. 250)) expressly obtained as to-

(i)   the nature and extent of the risk of diminution in the value of the assets in question, the type and specification of the derivatives suitable to reduce the impact of such diminution in value, and generally the strategy to be adopted in acquiring, holding and disposing of the derivatives;

(ii) the potential loss that could result from acquiring and holding the derivatives and the risk of such occurring; and

(iii) the nature and extent of the various risks of diminution in the value of the trust fund and the suitability of using derivatives to protect against those risks.

8. In this Schedule-

"authorized institution" has the meaning assigned to it in section 2 of the Banking Ordinance (Cap. 155);

"bill of exchange" and "promissory note" have the same meanings as in the Bills of Exchange Ordinance (Cap. 19);

"certificate of deposit" means a document relating to money, in any currency, which has been deposited with the issuer or some other person, being a document-

(a) which recognizes an obligation to pay a stated amount to bearer or to order, with or without interest; and

(b) by the delivery of which, with or without endorsement, the right to receive that stated amount, with or without interest, is transferable;

"company" means a body corporate-

(a) incorporated under the Companies Ordinance (Cap. 32);

(b) incorporated under any other enactment; or

(c) incorporated or established outside Hong Kong;

"debentures" includes debenture stock, bonds and any other securities of a company whether or not constituting a charge on the assets of the company;

"debt security" means-

(a) debenture or loan stock;

(b) debentures, bonds, notes and other securities or instruments

acknowledging, evidencing or creating indebtedness, whether secured or unsecured;

(c) options, warrants or similar rights to subscribe to or purchase any of the foregoing; and

(d) convertible loan stock;

"derivative" means any right in or to a financial contract or financial instrument the value of which is determined by reference to the value of or any fluctuation in the value of a share, index, rate of exchange or rate of interest either individually or in the aggregate;

"exempted body" means a body specified in Part IV or IVA of the Schedule to the Protection of Investors Ordinance (Cap. 335) but does not include any body listed in item 9 of Part IVA of that Schedule;

"shares" means shares in the capital of a company and includes the stock or any part of the stock of a company;

"Unified Exchange" has the meaning assigned to it by section 2(1) of the Stock Exchanges Unification Ordinance (Cap. 361).

TABLE

CREDIT RATINGS

(a)   For long-term debt (one year or over) -
Given by

Moody's Investors Service Inc.	A3
Standard & Poor's Corporation	A-

or an equivalent rating given by any recognized credit rating
agency approved by the Secretary for Financial Services.

(b)   For short-term debt (less than one year) -
Given by

Moody's Investors Service Inc.	Prime-1
Standard & Poor's Corporation	A-1

or an equivalent rating given by any recognized credit rating
agency approved by the Secretary for Financial Services.

VARIATION OF TRUSTS ORDINANCE

CHAPTER 253

To extend the jurisdiction of courts of law to vary trusts in the interests of the beneficiaries and to sanction dealings with trust property.

Short title

1.   This Ordinance may be cited as the Variation of Trusts Ordinance.

Interpretation

2.   In this Ordinance, unless the context otherwise requires-

"discretionary interest" means an interest arising under the trust specified in section 35(1)(b) of the Trustee Ordinance (Cap. 29) or any like trust;

"principal beneficiary" has the same meaning as in section 35 of the Trustee Ordinance (Cap. 29);

"protective trusts" means the trusts specified in section 35 of the Trustee Ordinance (Cap. 29) or any like trusts.

Jurisdiction of courts to vary trusts

3.(1)   Where property is held on trusts arising, whether before or after the commencement of this Ordinance, under any will, settlement or other disposition, the court may if it thinks fit by order approve on behalf of-

> *(a)*   any person having, directly or indirectly, an interest, whether vested or contingent, under the trusts who by reason of infancy or other incapacity is incapable of assenting; or
>
> *(b)*   any person (whether ascertained or not) who may be or may become entitled, directly or indirectly, to an interest under the trusts as being at a future date or on the happening of a future event a person of any specified description or a member of any specified class of persons, so however that this paragraph shall not include any person who would be of that description, or member of that class, as the case may be, if the said date had fallen or the said event had happened at the date of the application to the court; or
>
> *(c)*   any person unborn; or
>
> *(d)*   any person in respect of any discretionary interest of his under protective trusts where the interest of the principal beneficiary has not failed or determined,

any arrangement (by whomsoever proposed, and whether or not there is any other person beneficially interested who is capable of assenting thereto) varying or revoking all or any of the trusts, or enlarging the powers of the trustees of managing or administering any of the property subject to the trusts:

Provided that except by virtue of paragraph (d) the court shall not approve an arrangement on behalf of any person unless the carrying out thereof would be for the benefit of that person.

(2) Subject to the provisions of section 37(1)(b) of the District Court Ordinance (Cap. 336), the jurisdiction conferred by subsection (1) of this section shall be exercisable by the High Court.

(3) Nothing in this section shall apply to trusts affecting property settled by Ordinance.

(4) Nothing in this section shall be taken to limit the powers conferred by section 12(2) of the Supreme Court Ordinance (Cap. 4) or by section 56 of the Trustee Ordinance (Cap.29).

RECOGNITION OF TRUSTS ORDINANCE

Short title

1.   This Ordinance may be cited as the Recognition of Trusts Ordinance.

Applicable law and recognition of trusts

2.(1)   The provisions of the Convention set out in the Schedule shall have the force of law in Hong Kong.

(2) If there is any inconsistency between the text of the Convention in English as so set out and the text in Chinese, the text in English shall prevail.

(3) The provisions of the Convention shall, so far as applicable, have effect not only in relation to the trusts described in Articles 2 and 3 thereof but also in relation to any other trusts of property arising under the law of Hong Kong or by virtue of a judicial decision whether in Hong Kong or elsewhere.

(4) Where Articles 15 and 16 do not prevent the application of any provision of law, that provision of law shall, to the extent specified in Articles 15 and 16, apply notwithstanding anything to the contrary in any other Article of the Convention.

(5) In Article 17 the reference to a State includes a reference to any country or territory (whether or not a party to the Convention) which has its own system of law.

(6) Article 22 shall not be construed as affecting the law to be applied in relation to anything done or omitted before the coming into force of this Ordinance.

Application to the Crown

3.   This Ordinance shall bind the Crown.

SCHEDULE

Convention on The Law Applicable To Trusts

and on Their Recognition

Being The Convention A Draft Of Which Was Annexed To

The Final Act Of The Fifteenth Session Of The Hague

Conference On Private International Law Dated

At The Hague 20 October 1984 In English And

French, Both Texts Being Equally Authentic

CHAPTER I - Scope

Article 1

This Convention specifies the law applicable to trusts and governs their recognition.

Article 2

For the purposes of this Convention, the term "trust" refers to the legal relationship created - inter vivos or on death - by a person, the settlor, when assets have been placed under the control of a trustee for the benefit of a beneficiary or for a specified purpose.

A trust has the following characteristics-

(a) the assets constitute a separate fund and are not a part of the trustee's own estate;

(b) title to the trust assets stands in the name of the trustee or in the name of another person on behalf of the trustee;

(c) the trustee has the power and the duty, in respect of which he is accountable, to manage, employ or dispose of the assets in accordance with the terms of the trust and the special duties imposed upon him by law.

The reservation by the settlor of certain rights and powers, and the fact that the trustee may himself have rights as a beneficiary, are not necessarily inconsistent with the existence of a trust.

Article 3

The Convention applies only to trusts created voluntarily and evidenced in writing.

Article 4

The Convention does not apply to preliminary issues relating to the validity of wills or of other acts by virtue of which assets are transferred to the trustee.

Article 5

The Convention does not apply to the extent that the law specified by Chapter II does not provide for trusts or the category of trusts involved.

CHAPTER II - Applicable Law

Article 6

A trust shall be governed by the law chosen by the settlor. The choice must be express or be implied in the terms of the instrument creating or the writing evidencing the trust, interpreted, if necessary, in the light of the circumstances of the case.

Where the law chosen under the previous paragraph does not provide for trusts or the category of trust involved, the choice shall not be effective and the law specified in Article 7 shall apply.

Article 7

Where no applicable law has been chosen, a trust shall be governed by the law with which it is most closely connected.

In ascertaining the law with which a trust is most closely connected reference shall be made in particular to-

> *(a)* the place of administration of the trust designated by the settlor;
>
> *(b)* the situs of the assets of the trust;
>
> *(c)* the place of residence or business of the trustee;
>
> *(d)* the objects of the trust and the places where they are to be fulfilled.

Article 8

The law specified by Article 6 or 7 shall govern the validity of the trust, its construction, its effects and the administration of the trust.

In particular that law shall govern-

(a)   the appointment, resignation and removal of trustees, the capacity to act as a trustee, and the devolution of the office of trustee;

(b)   the rights and duties of trustees among themselves;

(c)   the right of trustees to delegate in whole or in part the discharge of their duties or the exercise of their powers;

(d)   the power of trustees to administer or to dispose of trust assets, to create security interests in the trust assets, or to acquire new assets;

(e)   the powers of investment of trustees;

(f)   restrictions upon the duration of the trust, and upon the power to accumulate the income of the trust;

(g)   the relationships between the trustees and the beneficiaries including the personal liability of the trustees to the beneficiaries;

(h)   the variation or termination of the trust;

(i)   the distribution of the trust assets;

(j)   the duty of trustees to account for their administration.

Article 9

In applying this Chapter a severable aspect of the trust, particularly matters of administration, may be governed by a different law.

Article 10

The law applicable to the validity of the trust shall determine whether that law or the law governing a severable aspect of the trust may be replaced by another law.

CHAPTER III - Recognition

Article 11

A trust created in accordance with the law specified by the preceding Chapter shall be recognized as a trust.

Such recognition shall imply, as a minimum, that the trust property constitutes a separate fund, that the trustee may sue and be sued in his capacity as trustee, and that he may appear or act in this capacity before a notary or any person acting in an official capacity.

In so far as the law applicable to the trust requires or provides, such recognition shall imply in particular-

> *(a)*   that personal creditors of the trustee shall have no recourse against the trust assets;

> *(b)*   that the trust assets shall not form part of the trustee's estate upon his insolvency or bankruptcy;

> *(c)*   that the trust assets shall not form part of the matrimonial property of the trustee or his spouse nor part of the trustee's estate upon his death;

> *(d)*   that the trust assets may be recovered when the trustee, in breach of trust, has mingled trust assets with his own property or has alienated trust assets. However, the rights and obligations of any third party holder of the assets shall remain subject to the law determined by the choice of law rules of the forum.

Article 12

Where the trustee desires to register assets, movable or immovable, or documents of title to them, he shall be entitled, in so far as this is not prohibited by or inconsistent with the law of the State where registration is sought, to do so in his capacity as trustee or in such other way that the existence of the trust is disclosed.

Article 14

The Convention shall not prevent the application of rules of law more favourable to the recognition of trusts.

CHAPTER IV- General Clauses

Article 15

The Convention does not prevent the application of provisions of the law designated by the conflicts rules of the forum, in so far as those provisions cannot be derogated from by voluntary act, relating in particular to the following matters-

> *(a)*   the protection of minors and incapable parties;
>
> *(b)*   the personal and proprietary effects of marriage;
>
> *(c)*   succession rights, testate and intestate, especially the indefeasible shares of spouses and relatives;
>
> *(d)*   the transfer of title to property and security interests in property;
>
> *(e)*   the protection of creditors in matters of insolvency;
>
> *(f)*   the protection, in other respects, of third parties acting in good faith.

If recognition of a trust is prevented by application of the preceding paragraph, the court shall try to give effect to the objects of the trust by other means.

Article 16

The Convention does not prevent the application of those provisions of the law of the forum which must be applied even to international situations, irrespective of rules of conflict of laws.

Article 17

In the Convention the word "law" means the rules of law in force in a State other than its rules of conflict of laws.

Article 18

The provisions of the Convention may be disregarded when their application would be manifestly incompatible with public policy.

Article 22

The Convention applies to trusts regardless of the date on which they were created.

PERPETUITIES AND ACCUMULATIONS ORDINANCE

CHAPTER 257

Preliminary and General

Perpetuities

Accumulations

To modify the law relating to the avoidance of future interests in property on grounds of remoteness and governing accumulations of income from property.

Preliminary and General

Short title

1.   This Ordinance may be cited as the Perpetuities and Accumulations Ordinance.

Interpretation

2.(1)   In this Ordinance, unless the context otherwise requires -

"disposition" includes the conferring of a power of appointment and any other disposition of an interest in or right over property, and references to the interest disposed of shall be construed accordingly;

"in being" means living or en ventre sa mere;

"power of appointment" includes any discretionary power to transfer a beneficial interest in property without the furnishing of valuable consideration;

"will" includes a codicil.

(2) For the purposes of this Ordinance a disposition contained in a will shall be deemed to be made at the death of the testator.

(3) For the purposes of this Ordinance a person shall be treated as a member of a class if in his case all the conditions identifying a member of the class are satisfied, and shall be treated as a potential member if in his case some only of those conditions are satisfied but there is a possibility that the remainder will in time be satisfied.

Application

3.(1)   Nothing in this Ordinance shall affect the operation of the rule of law rendering void for remoteness certain dispositions under which property is limited to be applied for purposes other than the benefit of any person or class of persons in cases where the property may be so applied after the end of the perpetuity period.

(2) This Ordinance shall apply (except as provided in subsection (2) of section 13 and section 18) only in relation to instruments taking effect after the commencement of this Ordinance, and in the case of an instrument made in the exercise of a special power of appointment shall apply only where the instrument creating the power takes effect after that commencement:

Provided that section 12 shall apply in all cases for construing the foregoing reference to a special power of appointment.

(3) This Ordinance shall apply in relation to a disposition made otherwise than by an instrument as if the disposition had been contained in an instrument taking effect when the disposition was made.

(4) This Ordinance binds the Crown.

Perpetuities

Abolition of the double possibility rule

4. The rule of law prohibiting the limitation, after a life interest to an unborn person, of an interest in land to the unborn child or other issue of an unborn person is hereby abolished, but without prejudice to any other rule relating to perpetuities.

Restrictions on the perpetuity rule

5. For removing doubts, it is hereby declared that the rule of law relating to perpetuities does not apply and shall be deemed never to have applied-

> *(a)* to any power to distrain on or to take possession of land or the income thereof given by way of indemnity against a rent, whether charged upon or payable in respect of any part of that land or not; or

> *(b)* to any grant, exception, or reservation of any right of entry on, or user of, the surface of land or of any easements, rights, or privileges over or under land for the purpose of-

>> **(i)** executing repairs, alterations, or additions to any adjoining land, or the buildings and erections thereon;

>> **(ii)** constructing, laying down, altering, repairing, renewing, cleansing, and maintaining sewers, watercourses, cesspools, gutters, drains, water-pipes, gas-pipes, electric wires or cables or other like works.

Power to specify perpetuity period

6.(1) Subject to subsection (2) of section 14 and subsection (2) of this section, where the instrument by which any disposition is made so provides, the perpetuity period applicable to the disposition under the rule against perpetuities, instead of being of any other duration, shall be of a duration equal to such number of years not exceeding eighty as is specified in that behalf in the instrument.

(2) Subsection (1) shall not have effect where the disposition is made in exercise of a special power of appointment, but where a period is specified under that subsection in the instrument creating such a power the period shall apply in relation to any disposition under the power as it applies in relation to the power itself.

Presumptions and evidence as to future parenthood

7.(1) Where in any proceedings there arises on the rule against perpetuities a question which turns on the ability of a person to have a child at some future time, then-

(a) subject to paragraph (b), it shall be presumed that a male can have a child at the age of fourteen years or over, but not under that age, and that a female can have a child at the age of twelve years or over, but not under that age or over the age of fifty-five years; but

(b) in the case of a living person evidence may be given to show that he or she will or will not be able to have a child at the time in question.

(2) Where any such question is decided by treating a person as unable to have a child at a particular time, and he or she does so, the High Court may make such order as it thinks fit for placing the persons interested in the property comprised in the disposition, so far as may be just, in the position they would have held if the question had not been so decided.

(3) Subject to subsection (2), where any such question is decided in relation to a disposition by treating a person as able or unable to have a child at a particular time, then he or she shall be so treated for the purpose of any question which may arise on the rule against perpetuities in relation to the same disposition in any subsequent proceedings.

(4) In the foregoing provisions of this section references to having a child are references to begetting or giving birth to a child, but those provisions (except paragraph (b) of subsection (1)) shall apply in relation to the possibility that a person will at any time have a child by adoption, legitimation or other means as they apply to his or her ability at that time to beget or give birth to a child.

Uncertainty as to remoteness

8.(1) Where, apart from the provisions of this section and sections 9 and 10, a disposition would be void on the ground that the interest disposed of might not become vested until too remote a time, the disposition shall be treated, until such time (if any) as it becomes established that the vesting must occur, if at all, after the end of the perpetuity period, as if the disposition were not subject to the rule against perpetuities; and its becoming so established shall not affect the validity of anything previously done in relation to the interest disposed of by way of advancement, application of intermediate income or otherwise.

(2) Where, apart from the said provisions, a disposition consisting of the conferring of a general power of appointment would be void on the ground that the power might not become exercisable until too remote a time, the disposition shall be treated, until such time (if any) as it becomes established that the power will not be exercisable within the perpetuity period, as if the disposition were not subject to the rule against perpetuities.

(3) Where, apart from the said provisions, a disposition consisting of the conferring of any power, option or other right would be void on the ground that the right might be exercised at too remote a time, the disposition shall be treated as regards any exercise of the right within the perpetuity period as if it were not subject to the rule against perpetuities, and, subject to the said provisions, shall be treated as void for remoteness only if, and so far as, the right is not fully exercised within that period.

(4) Where this section applies to a disposition and the duration of the perpetuity period is not determined by virtue of section 6 or subsection (2) of section 14, it shall be determined as follows

    (a)   where any persons falling within subsection (5) are individuals in being and ascertainable at the commencement of the perpetuity period the duration of the period shall be determined by reference to their lives and no others, but so that the lives of any description of persons falling within paragraph (b) or (c) of that subsection shall be disregarded if the number of persons of that description is such as to render it impracticable to ascertain the date of death of the survivor;

    (b)   where there are no lives under paragraph (a) the period shall be twenty-one years.

(5)   The said persons are as follows-

    (a)   the person by whom the disposition was made;

    (b)   a person to whom or in whose favour the disposition was made, that is to say-

        (i)   in the case of a disposition to a class of persons, any member or potential member of the class;

        (ii)   in the case of an individual disposition to a person taking only on certain conditions being satisfied, any person as to whom some of the conditions are satisfied and the remainder may in time be satisfied;

        (iii)   in the case of a special power of appointment exercisable in favour of members of a class, any member or potential member of the class;

        (iv)   in the case of a special power of appointment exercisable in favour of one person only, that person or, where the object of the power is ascertainable only on certain conditions being satisfied, any person as to whom some of the conditions are satisfied and the remainder may in time be satisfied;

        (v)   in the case of any power, option or other right, the person on whom the right is conferred;

(c) a person having a child or grandchild within sub-paragraphs (i) to (iv) of paragraph (b), or any of whose children or grandchildren, if subsequently born, would by virtue of his or her descent fall within those sub-paragraphs;

(d) any person on the failure or determination of whose prior interest the disposition is limited to take effect.

Reduction of age and exclusion of class members to avoid remoteness

9.(1) Where a disposition is limited by reference to the attainment by any person or persons of a specified age exceeding twenty-one years, and it is apparent at the time the disposition is made or becomes apparent at a subsequent time-

(a) that the disposition would, apart from this section, be void for remoteness; but

(b) that it would not be so void if the specified age had been twenty-one years,

the disposition shall be treated for all purposes as if, instead of being limited by reference to the age in fact specified, it had been limited by reference to the age nearest to that age which would, if specified instead, have prevented the disposition from being so void.

(2) Where in the case of any disposition different ages exceeding twenty-one years are specified in relation to different persons-

(a) the reference in paragraph (b) of subsection (1) to the specified age shall be construed as a reference to all the specified ages; and

(b) that subsection shall operate to reduce each such age so far as is necessary to save the disposition from being void for remoteness.

(3) Where the inclusion of any persons, being potential members of a class or unborn persons who at birth would become members or potential members of the class, prevents the foregoing provisions of this section from operating to save a disposition from being void for remoteness, those persons shall thenceforth be deemed for all the purposes of the disposition to be excluded from the class, and the said provisions shall thereupon have effect accordingly.

(4) Where, in the case of a disposition to which subsection (3) does not apply, it is apparent at the time the disposition is made or becomes apparent at a subsequent time, that apart from this subsection, the inclusion of any persons, being potential members of a class or unborn persons who at birth would become members or potential members of the class, would cause the disposition to be treated as void for remoteness, those persons shall, unless their exclusion would exhaust the class, thenceforth be deemed for all the purposes of the disposition to be excluded from the class.

(5) Where this section has effect in relation to a disposition to which section 8 applies, the operation of this section shall not affect the validity of anything previously done in relation to the interest disposed of by way of advancement, application of intermediate income or otherwise.

Condition relating to death of surviving spouse

10. Where a disposition is limited by reference to the time of death of the survivor of a person in being at the commencement of the perpetuity period and any spouse of that person, and that time has not arrived at the end of the perpetuity period, the disposition shall be treated for all purposes, where to do so would save it from being void for remoteness, as if it had instead been limited by reference to the time immediately before the end of that period.

Saving and acceleration of expectant interests

11. A disposition shall not be treated as void for remoteness by reason only that the interest disposed of is ulterior to and dependent upon an interest under a disposition which is so void, and the vesting of an interest shall not be prevented from being accelerated on the failure of a prior interest by reason only that the failure arises because of remoteness.

Powers of appointment

12. For the purposes of the rule against perpetuities, a power of appointment shall be treated as a special power unless

> *(a)* in the instrument creating the power it is expressed to be exercisable by one person only; and

> *(b)* it could, at all times during its currency when that person is of full age and capacity, be exercised by him so as immediately to transfer to himself the whole of the interest governed by the power without the consent of any other person or compliance with any other condition, not being a formal condition relating only to the mode of exercise of the power:

Provided that for the purpose of determining whether a disposition made under a power of appointment exercisable by will only is void for remoteness, the power shall be treated as a general power where it would have fallen to be so treated if exercisable by deed.

Administrative powers of trustees

13.(1) The rule against perpetuities shall not operate to invalidate a power conferred on trustees or other persons to sell, lease, exchange or otherwise dispose of any property for full consideration, or to do any other act in the administration (as opposed to the distribution) of any property, and shall not prevent the payment to trustees or other persons of reasonable remuneration for their services.

(2) Subsection (1) shall apply for the purpose of enabling a power to be exercised at any time after the commencement of this Ordinance notwithstanding that the power is conferred by an instrument which took effect before that commencement.

Options relating to land

14.(1) The rule against perpetuities shall not apply to a disposition consisting of the conferring of an option to acquire for valuable consideration an interest reversionary (whether directly or indirectly) on the term of a lease if-

        (a)   the option is exercisable only by the lessee or his successors in title; and

        (b)   it ceases to be exercisable at or before the expiration of one year following the determination of the lease.

This subsection shall apply in relation to an agreement for a lease as it applies in relation to a lease, and "lessee" shall be construed accordingly.

(2) In the case of a disposition consisting of the conferring of an option to acquire for valuable consideration any interest in land, the perpetuity period under the rule against perpetuities shall be twenty-one years, and section 6 shall not apply.

Avoidance of contractual and other rights in cases of remoteness

15. Where a disposition inter vivos would fall to be treated as void for remoteness if the rights and duties thereunder were capable of transmission to persons other than the original parties and had been so transmitted, it shall be treated as void as between the person by whom it was made and the person to whom or in whose favour it was made or any successor of his, and no remedy shall lie in contract or otherwise for giving effect to it or making restitution for its lack of effect.

Possibilities of resulting trust, conditions subsequent, exceptions and reservations

16.(1) In the case of a possibility of a resulting trust on the determination of any determinable interest in property, the rule against perpetuities shall apply in relation to the provision causing the interest to be determinable as it would apply if that provision were expressed in the form of a condition subsequent giving rise, on breach thereof, to a right of re-entry or an equivalent right in the case of property other than land, and where the provision falls to be treated as void for remoteness the determinable interest shall become an absolute interest.

(2) Where a disposition is subject to any such provision, or to any such condition subsequent, or to any exception or reservation, the disposition shall be treated for the purposes of this Ordinance as including a separate disposition of any rights arising by virtue of the provision, condition subsequent, exception or reservation.

Accumulations

General restrictions on accumulations of income

17.(1) No person may by any instrument or otherwise settle or dispose of any property in such manner that the income thereof shall, save as hereinafter mentioned, be wholly or partially accumulated for any longer period than one of the following, namely-

(a)   the life of the grantor or settlor; or

(b)   a term of twenty-one years from the death of the grantor, settlor or testator; or

(c)   the duration of the minority or respective minorities of any person in being at the death of the grantor, settlor or testator; or

(d)   the duration of the minority or respective minorities only of any person who under the limitations of the instrument directing the accumulations would, for the time being, if of full age, be entitled to the income directed to be accumulated; or

(e)   a term of twenty-one years from the date of the making of the disposition; or

(f)   the duration of the minority or respective minorities of any person or persons in being at the date of the making of the disposition.

(2) In every case where any accumulation is directed otherwise than as aforesaid, the direction shall (save as hereinafter mentioned) be void; and the income of the property directed to be accumulated shall, so long as the same is directed to be accumulated contrary to this section, go to and be received by the person who would have been entitled thereto if such accumulation had not been directed.

(3) The restrictions imposed by subsection (1) apply in relation to a power to accumulate income whether or not there is a duty to exercise that power, and they apply whether or not the power to accumulate extends to income produced by the investment of income previously accumulated.

(4) This section does not extend to any provision-

(a)   for payment of the debts of any grantor, settlor, testator or other person;

(b)   for raising portions for-

(i)   any child or remoter issue of any grantor, settlor or testator; or

(ii)   any child or remoter issue of a person taking any interest under any settlement or other disposition directing the accumulations or to whom any interest is thereby limited,

and accordingly such provisions may be made as if no statutory restrictions on accumulation of income had been imposed.

Qualification of restrictions on accumulation

18. Where accumulations of surplus income are made during a minority under any Ordinance or under the general law, the period for which such accumulations are made is not (whether the trust was created or the accumulations were made before or after the commencement of this Ordinance) to be taken into account in determining the periods for which accumulations are permitted to be made by section 17, and accordingly an express trust for accumulation for any other permitted period shall not be deemed to have been invalidated or become invalid, by reason of accumulations also having been made as aforesaid during such minority.

Restriction on accumulation for the purchase of land

19. No person may settle or dispose of any property in such manner that the income thereof shall be wholly or partially accumulated for the purchase of land only, for any longer period than the duration of the minority or respective minorities of any person or persons who, under the limitations of the instrument directing the accumulation, would for the time being, if of full age, be entitled to the income so directed to be accumulated.

Right to stop accumulations

20. Section 7 shall apply to any question as to the right of beneficiaries to put an end to accumulations of income under any disposition as it applies to questions arising on the rule against perpetuities.

INTERPRETATION AND GENERAL CLAUSES ORDINANCE

CONTENTS

Part I - Short Title and Application

Part II - Interpretation of Words and Expressions

Part IIA - General Provisions as to Laws in Both Official Languages

Part III - General Provisions as To Ordinances

Part IV - Commencement, Disallowance, Amendment and Repeal

Part VIII - Public Officers and Public Contracts

Part IX - Crown, Governor and Governor In Council

Part X - Time and Distance

Part XI - Imperial Enactments

Part XII - (*Repealed*)

Part XIII - Miscellaneous

CHAPTER 1

INTERPRETATION AND GENERAL CLAUSES

To consolidate and amend the law relating to the construction, application and interpretation of laws, to make general provisions with regard thereto, to define terms and expressions used in laws and public documents, to make general provision with regard to public officers, public contracts and civil and criminal proceedings and for purposes and for matters incidental thereto or connected therewith.

PART I - Short Title And Application

Short title

1. This Ordinance may be cited as the Interpretation and General ClausesOrdinance.

Application

2.(1)   Save where the contrary intention appears either from this Ordinance or from the context of any other Ordinance or instrument, the provisions of this Ordinance shall apply to this Ordinance and to any other Ordinance in force, whether such other Ordinance came or comes into operation before or after the commencement of this Ordinance, and to any instrument made or issued under or by virtue of any such Ordinance.

(1A) The inclusion of the substance of a provision of this Ordinance in another Ordinance does not imply the exclusion of the application of any other provision of this Ordinance to the other Ordinance.

(2) This Ordinance shall be binding on the Crown.

PART II - Interpretation of Words and Expressions

Interpretation of words and expressions

3.   "act", when used with reference to an offence or civil wrong, includes a series of acts, an illegal omission and a series of illegal omissions;

"Administrative Appeals Board" means the Administrative Appeals Board established under the Administrative Appeals Board Ordinance (Cap. 442);

"adult" means a person who has attained the age of 18 years;

"aircraft" means any machine that can derive support in the atmosphere from the reactions of the air;

"alien" means a person who is neither a Commonwealth citizen nor a British protected person nor a citizen of the Republic of Ireland;

"amend" includes repeal, add to or vary and the doing of all or any of such things simultaneously or by the same Ordinance or instrument;

"arrestable offence" means an offence for which the sentence is fixed by law or for which a person may under or by virtue of any law be sentenced to imprisonment for a term exceeding 12 months, and an attempt to commit any such offence;

"Attorney General" means the Attorney General of Hong Kong;

"British citizen" means a person who has the status of a British citizen under the British Nationality Act 1981 (1981 c. 61 U.K.);

"British Dependent Territories citizen" means a person who has the status of a British Dependent Territories citizen under the British Nationality Act 1981 (1981 c.61 U.K.);

"British Overseas citizen" means a person who has the status of a British Overseas citizen under the British Nationality Act 1981 (1981 c.61 U.K.);

"British protected person" means a person who has the status of a British protected person under the British Nationality Act 1981 (1981 c.61 U.K.);

"British subject" means a person who has the status of a British subject under the British Nationality Act 1981 (1981 c. 61 U.K.);

"Chief Justice" means the Chief Justice of Hong Kong;

"Chief Secretary" means the Chief Secretary of Hong Kong;

"Clerk to the Executive Council" includes any person appointed by the Governor to be Deputy Clerk to the Executive Council;

"Clerk to the Legislative Council" means the Secretary General of the Legislative Council Secretariat appointed under section 15(1) of The Legislative Council Commission Ordinance (Cap. 443) and includes the

Deputy Secretary General and any Assistant Secretary General of the Legislative Council Secretariat;

"Colony" and "Hong Kong" mean the area of land and the area of Deep Bay and Mirs Bay lying within the boundaries specified in Schedule 2 and the territorial waters appertaining thereto;

"commencement", when used in relation to an Ordinance, or any part or provision thereof, means the date on which the Ordinance, part or provision came or comes into operation;

"committed for trial", when used in relation to any person, means-

> *(a)*   committed to prison with a view to his being tried before the High Court; or

> *(b)*   admitted to bail upon recognizances to appear and stand his trial before the High Court;

"common law" means the common law of England;

"Commonwealth citizen" means a person who has the status of a

Commonwealth citizen under the British Nationality Act 1981 (1981 c. 61 U.K.);

"consul" and "consular officer" mean any person, including the head of a consular post, recognized by the competent authority of the receiving state as entrusted in that capacity with the exercise of consular functions;

"contravene" in relation to any requirement or condition prescribed in any Ordinance or in any grant, permit, licence, lease or authority granted under or by virtue of any Ordinance includes a failure to comply with that requirement or condition;

"counsel" means a person admitted to practise as counsel before the High Court;

"court" means any court of the Colony of competent jurisdiction;
"Crown Agents" means the persons or body for the time being acting as Crown Agents for

Oversea Governments and Administrations;

"Crown lease" means any lease granted by the Crown, any instrument whereby the term of a Crown lease may have been extended or the provisions thereof varied and any agreement for a Crown lease;

"District Board" means a District Board established under the District Boards Ordinance (Cap.366);

"District Court" means the District Court of Hong Kong;

"District Judge" means a judge of the District Court;

"document" means any publication and any matter written, expressed or described upon any substance by means of letters, characters, figures or marks, or by more than one of these means;

"Executive Council" means the Executive Council of Hong Kong;

"export" means to take out or cause to be taken out of the Colony by air, land or water;

"Financial Secretary" means the Financial Secretary of Hong Kong and the Secretary for the Treasury;

"financial year" means the period from 1 April in any year to 31 March in the immediately succeeding year, both days inclusive;

"full age" means the age of 18 years;

"Gazette" means-

   (a)   the Hong Kong Government Gazette and any supplement
           thereto;

   (b)   the Hong Kong (British Military Administration) Gazette
           published on or between 12 October 1945 and 1 May 1946; and

   (c)   any Special Gazette or Gazette Extraordinary;

"general revenue" means the general revenue of Hong Kong;

"Government" means the Government of Hong Kong;

"Government Printer" means the Government Printer of Hong Kong and any other printer authorized by or on behalf of the Governor to print any Ordinance or any other document of the Government;

"Governor" means-

(a)   the Governor of Hong Kong;

(b)   the Acting Governor;

(c)   to the extent to which a deputy to the Governor is authorized to perform on behalf of the Governor any functions of the Governor, the Deputy to the Governor; and

(d)   where the Governor of Hong Kong is not intended, the Governor General, Governor, administrator or other officer for the time being administering the government of any British possession;

"Governor in Council", "Governor in Executive Council" and "Governor with the advice of the Executive Council" mean the Governor acting after consultation with the Executive Council in accordance with Royal Instructions but not necessarily in such Council assembled;

"Harbour" means the waters of the Colony within the boundaries specified in Schedule 3;

"health officer" means-

(a)   the Director, Deputy Director and Assistant Director of Health;

(b)   any person appointed as a health officer by the Governor; and

(c)   any person for the time being performing the duties of a health officer under any Ordinance;

"immovable property" means-

(a)   land, whether covered by water or not;

(b)   any estate, right, interest or easement in or over any land; and

(c)   things attached to land or permanently fastened to anything attached to land;

"imperial enactment" means-

(a)   any Act of Parliament;

(b)   any Order in Council;

(c)   any Letters Patent or Royal Instructions; and

(d)   any rule, regulation, proclamation, order, notice, rule of court, by-law or other instrument made under or by virtue of any Act, Order in Council, Letters Patent or Royal Instructions;

"import" means to bring or cause to be brought into the Colony by air, land or water;

"infant" and "minor" mean a person who has not attained the age of 18 years;

"instrument" includes any publication in the Gazette having legal effect;

"judge" means the Chief Justice, a Justice of Appeal, a judge of the High Court of Justice, a recorder of the High Court of Justice and a deputy judge of the High Court of Justice;

"justice" and "justice of the peace" mean a person appointed to be a justice of the peace for the Colony either by the Governor or by or under any Ordinance;

"Kowloon" means the area specified in Schedule 4;

"Lands Tribunal" means the Lands Tribunal established under section 3 of the Lands Tribunal Ordinance (Cap. 17);

"law" means any law for the time being in force in, having legislative effect in, extending to, or applicable in, the Colony;

"Legislative Council" means the Legislative Council of Hong Kong;

"magistrate" means-

(a)   any person appointed to be a permanent or special magistrate under the Magistrates Ordinance (Cap. 227); and

(b)   2 justices of the peace sitting together, to whom section 7(2) of the Magistrates Ordinance (Cap. 227) applies;

"master", when used with reference to a vessel, means the person (except a pilot) having for the time being command or charge of the vessel;

"medical practitioner", "registered medical practitioner" and any words importing that a person is recognized by any Ordinance to be a medical practitioner in Hong Kong or a member of the medical profession in Hong Kong, mean a person duly registered as, or deemed to be registered as, a medical practitioner under the Medical Registration Ordinance (Cap. 161);

"month" means calendar month;

"movable property" means property of every description except immovable property;

"New Kowloon" means the area specified in Schedule 5;

"New Territories" means the territories leased to Great Britain by the Emperor of China under the Convention dated 9 June 1898;

"oath" and "affidavit" include, in the case of persons allowed or required by law to affirm instead of swearing, affirmation; and "swear" in the like case includes affirm;

"occupy" includes use, inhabit, be in possession of or enjoy the land or premises to which the word relates, otherwise than as a mere servant or for the mere purpose of the care, custody or charge thereof;

"offence" includes any crime and any contravention or other breach of, or failure to comply with, any provision of any Ordinance, for which a penalty is provided;

"official languages" means the English language and the Chinese Language, and a reference to an "official language" shall be construed as a reference to the English language or the Chinese language as the case may be;

"Order in Council" means an order made by Her Majesty in Her Privy Council;

"Ordinance" and "enactment" mean-

> *(a)* any Ordinance enacted by the Governor by and with the advice and consent of the Legislative Council;

> *(b)* any proclamation made by the British Military Administration on or between 1 September 1945 and I May 1946; and

> *(c)* any subsidiary legislation made under any such Ordinance or proclamation;

"Parliament" and "Imperial Parliament" mean the Parliament of England, the Parliament of Great Britain and the Parliament of the United Kingdom;

"per cent", when used in relation to a rate of interest payable in any circumstances, means the rate of interest specified payable in respect of a year, unless it is expressly provided that it is payable in respect of any other period;

"person" includes any public body and any body of persons, corporate or unincorporate, and this definition shall apply notwithstanding that the word "person" occurs in a provision creating or relating to an offence or for the recovery of any fine or compensation;

"pier" includes every quay, wharf or jetty of whatever description connected to and having direct access to the shore and used or intended to be used for the purposes of a pier, quay, wharf or jetty;

"police officer" and terms or expression referring to ranks in the Royal Hong Kong Police Force shall bear the meanings respectively assigned to them by the Police Force Ordinance (Cap.232);

"power" includes any privilege, authority and discretion;

"prescribed" and "provided", when used in or with reference to any Ordinance, mean prescribed or provided by that Ordinance or by subsidiary legislation made under that Ordinance;

"prison" means any place or building or portion of a building set apart for the purpose of a prison under any Ordinance relating to prisons;

"Privy Council" means the Lords and others for the time being of Her Majesty's Most Honourable Privy Council;

"property" includes-

    (a)   money, goods, choses in action and land; and

    (b)   obligations, easements and every description of estate, interest and profit, present or future, vested or contingent, arising out of or incident to property as defined in paragraph (a) of this

        definition;

"public" includes any class of the public;

"publication" means-

    (a)   all written and printed matter;

    (b)   any record, tape, wire, perforated roll, cinematograph film or other contrivance by means of which any words or ideas may be mechanically, electronically or electrically produced, reproduced, represented or conveyed;

    (c)   anything whether of a similar nature to the foregoing or not, containing any visible representation, or by its form, shape, or in any manner, capable of producing, reproducing, representing or conveying words or ideas; and

    (d)   every copy and reproduction of any publication as defined in paragraphs (a), (b) and (c) of this definition;

"public body" includes-

    (a)   the Executive Council;

    (b)   the Legislative Council;

    (c)   the Urban Council;

        (ca)   any District Board;

        (cb)   the Regional Council;

    (d)   any other urban, rural or municipal council;

    (e)   any department of the Government; and

    (f)   any undertaking by or of the Government;

"public holiday" and "general holiday" mean any day which is a general holiday by virtue of any provision of the Holidays Ordinance (Cap. 149);

"public office" means any office or employment the holding or discharging of which by a person would constitute that person a public officer;

"public officer" and "public servant" mean any person holding an office of emolument under the Crown in right of the Government of Hong Kong, whether such office be permanent or temporary;

"public place" means-

    (a)   any public street or pier, or any public garden; and

    (b)   any theatre, place of public entertainment of any kind, or other place of general resort, admission to which is obtained by payment or to which the public have or are permitted to have access;

"public seal" means the public seal of Hong Kong;

"Regional Council" means the Regional Council established by the Regional Council Ordinance (Cap.385);

"registered", when used with reference to a document, means registered under the provisions of any law applicable to the registration of such a document;

"Registrar of the Supreme Court" means the Registrar of the Supreme Court and any Deputy or Assistant Registrar of the Supreme Court;

"repeal" includes rescind, revoke, cancel or replace;

"rules of court", when used in relation to any court, means rules made by the authority having for the time being power to make rules and orders regulating the practice and procedure of such court;

"Secretary of State" means one of Her Majesty's Principal Secretaries of State for the time being;

"sell" includes exchange and barter;

"ship" includes every description of vessel used in navigation not exclusively propelled by oars;

"sign" includes, in the case of a person unable to write, the affixing or making of a seal, mark, thumbprint or chop;

"solicitor" means a person admitted to practise as a solicitor before the High Court;

"statutory declaration", if made-

    (a)   in Hong Kong, means a declaration under the *Repealed* Statutory Declarations Ordinance or the Oaths and Declarations Ordinance (Cap.11);

(b)   in any part of the Commonwealth except the Colony, means a declaration made before a justice of the peace, notary public, or other person having authority therein under any legal provision for the time being in force in such part to take or receive a declaration;

(c)   in any other place, means a declaration before a British consul or person having authority under any Act for the time being in force to take or receive a declaration;

"street" and "road" mean-

(a)   any highway, street, road, bridge, thoroughfare, parade, square, court, alley, lane, bridle-way, footway, passage, tunnel; and

(b)   any open place, whether situate on land leased from the Crown or not, used or frequented by the public or to which the public have or are permitted to have access;

"subsidiary legislation" and "regulations" mean any proclamation, rule, regulation, order, resolution, notice, rule of court, bylaw or other instrument made under or by virtue of any Ordinance and having legislative effect;

"summary conviction" means a summary conviction by a magistrate in accordance with the provisions of the Magistrates Ordinance (Cap. 227);

"Supreme Court" means the Supreme Court of Hong Kong;

"surname" includes a clan or family name;

"territorial waters" means such part of the sea adjacent to the coast of the Colony as is deemed by international law to constitute the territorial waters of Hong Kong;

"treaty" means a treaty, convention or agreement made with a foreign state, and any protocol or declaration attached thereto or independent thereof but referring thereto;

"triable summarily" means triable by a magistrate, in accordance with the of the Magistrates Ordinance (Cap. 227);

"trust territory" means a territory administered by the Government of any part of Her Majesty's dominions under the trusteeship system of the United Nations;
"United Kingdom" means-

(a)   the United Kingdom of Great Britain and Northern Ireland; or

> (b) when used with reference to citizenship or nationality, Great Britain, Northern Ireland, the Channel Islands and the Isle of Man;

"Urban Council" means the Urban Council established by the Urban Council Ordinance (Cap. 101);

"vessel" means any ship or boat and any description of vessel used in navigation;

"Victoria" means the area within the boundaries specified in Schedule 1;

"waters of the Colony", "waters of Hong Kong and "Colonial waters" mean

> (a) all waters, whether navigable or not, included in the Colony; and

> (b) territorial waters;

"words" includes figures and symbols;

"writing" and "printing" include writing, printing, lithography, photography, typewriting and any other mode of representing words in a visible form;

"year" means a year according to the Gregorian calendar;

"years of age" and words of a like meaning, when used with reference to the age of any person, mean years of age according to the English reckoning of ages.

Definition of "Commonwealth"

4. "Commonwealth" means collectively-

> (a) the United Kingdom;

> (b) the Channel Islands;

> (c) the Isle of Man;

> (d) the countries mentioned in Schedule 3 to the British Nationality Act 1981 (1981 c. 61 U.K.);

> (e) the British Dependent Territories mentioned in Schedule 6 to the British Nationality Act 1981 (1981 c. 61 U.K.).

Grammatical variations and cognate expressions

5. Where any word or expression is defined in any Ordinance, such definition shall extend to the grammatical variations and cognate expressions of such word or expression.

References to Government property

6. Where reference is made in any Ordinance to property and the expressions used in relation thereto imply that such property is owned by, or belongs to, the Government, or convey a similar meaning, such reference shall be deemed to refer to such of the property of the Crown of the description mentioned as has been appropriated to the use of the Government.

Provisions for gender and number

7.(1) Words and expressions importing the masculine gender include the feminine and neuter genders.

(2) Words and expressions in the singular include the plural and words and expressions in the plural include the singular.

Service by post

8. Where any Ordinance authorizes or requires any documents to be served or any notice to be given by post or by registered post, whether the expression "serve" or "give" or "send" or any other expression is used, the service or notice shall be deemed to be effected by properly addressing, pre-paying the postage thereon and dispatching it by post or by registered post, as the case may be, to the last known postal address of the person to be served or given notice, and, unless the contrary is proved, such service or notice shall be deemed to have been effected at the time at which the document or notice would be delivered in the ordinary course of post.

Chinese words and expressions

9. Chinese words and expressions in the English text of an Ordinance shall be construed according to Chinese language and custom.

References to pounds sterling

10. The amount of Hong Kong dollars equivalent to an amount of pounds sterling referred to in any law shall be calculated at the merchant selling rate of The Hong Kong Association of Banks at the close of business on the relevant day.

PART IIA - General Provisions as To Laws in Both Official Languages

Application of Part IIA

10A. This Part shall apply to an Ordinance-

(a) enacted in both official languages; or

(b) in respect of which an authentic text is published under section 4B of the Official Languages Ordinance (Cap. 5).

Construction of Ordinances in both official languages

10B.(1) The English language text and the Chinese language text of an Ordinance shall be equally authentic, and the Ordinance shall be construed accordingly.

(2) The provisions of an Ordinance are presumed to have the same meaning in each authentic text.

(3) Where a comparison of the authentic texts of an Ordinance discloses a difference of meaning which the rules of statutory interpretation ordinarily applicable do not resolve, the meaning which best reconciles the texts, having regard to the object and purposes of the Ordinance, shall be adopted.

Expressions of English law

10C.(1) Where an expression of the common law is used in the English language text of an Ordinance and an analogous expression is used in the Chinese language text thereof, the Ordinance shall be construed in accordance with the common law meaning of that expression.

(2) In this section "common law" means the common law and rules of equity in force in Hong Kong.

Name of statutory body corporate

10D. Where an Ordinance establishes a body corporate and in the English language text and Chinese language text of that Ordinance the name of the body corporate is in the form only of the language of that text, the name of the body corporate shall consist of the form of its name in each of the texts of the Ordinance.

Words etc. in the official languages may be declared as equivalents

10E.(1) The Governor in Council may, by notice in the Gazette, declare that any word, expression, office, title (including the short title of any Ordinance), citation or thing therein specified in one official language shall, in relation to the interpretation of an Ordinance, be the equivalent of any word, expression, office, title, citation or thing therein specified in the other official language.

(2) No declaration shall be made under this section unless a draft of the notice has been laid before and approved by resolution of the Legislative Council, and section 34 of this Ordinance shall not apply in relation to any such declaration.

PART III - General Provisions as To Ordinances

Ordinance to be public Ordinance

11. Every Ordinance shall be a public Ordinance and shall be judicially noticed as such.

12. (*Repealed*)

Citation of Ordinance

13.(1) Where any Ordinance is referred to, it shall be sufficient for all purposes to cite such Ordinance by-

> *(a)* the title, short title or citation thereof,
>
> *(b)* its number among the Ordinances of the year in which it was enacted; or
>
> *(c)* any chapter number lawfully given to it under the authority of any Ordinance providing for the issue of a revised or other edition of the laws of Hong Kong.

(2) Any reference made to any Ordinance, in accordance with the provisions of subsection (1), may be made according to the title, short title, citation, number or chapter number used in copies of Ordinances printed by the Government Printer.

14. (*Repealed*)

Reference to Ordinance as amended

15.(1) Where in any Ordinance a reference is made to another Ordinance, such reference shall be deemed to include a reference to such last mentioned Ordinance as the same may from time to time be amended.

(2) Where any Ordinance repeals and re-enacts, with or without modification, any provision of a former Ordinance, references in any other Ordinance to the provision so *Repealed* shall be construed as references to the provision so re-enacted.

Citation of part of Ordinance

16. In any Ordinance a description or citation of a portion of an Ordinanceshall be construed as including the word, section or other part mentioned or referred to as forming the beginning and as forming the end of the portion comprised in the description or citation.

Construction of reference to Ordinance, section, etc.

17.(1) Any reference in any Ordinance to "any Ordinance" or to "any enactment" shall be construed as a reference to any Ordinance for the time being in force.

(2) Where in an Ordinance there is a reference to a section or other division by number, letter or combination of number and letter, and not in conjunction with the title or short title of any other Ordinance, the reference shall be construed as a reference to the section or other division of that number, letter or combination in the Ordinance in which the reference occurs.

(3) Where in a section of an Ordinance there is a reference to a subsection or other division by number, letter or combination of number and letter, and not in conjunction with the number of a section of that or any other Ordinance, the reference shall be construed as a reference to the subsection or other division of that number, letter or combination in the section in which the reference occurs.

(4)-(5) *(Repealed)*

Marginal notes and section headings

18.(1) Where any section, subsection or paragraph of any Ordinance is taken verbatim from, or is substantially similar to, a section, subsection or paragraph of any imperial enactment, there may be added as a note to the section, subsection or paragraph of the Ordinance a reference, in abbreviated form, to such section, subsection or paragraph of the imperial enactment.

(2) A reference added under subsection (1) shall not have any legislative effect and shall not in any way vary, limit or extend the interpretation of any Ordinance.

(3) A marginal note or section heading to any provision of any Ordinance shall not have any legislative effect and shall not in any way vary, limit or extend the interpretation of any Ordinance.

General principles of interpretation

19. An Ordinance shall be deemed to be remedial and shall receive such fair, large and liberal construction and interpretation as will best ensure the attainment of the object of the Ordinance according to its true intent, meaning and spirit.

PART IV - Commencement, Disallowance, Amendment And Repeal

Commencement, etc., of Ordinance

20.(1) An Ordinance shall be published in the Gazette.

(2) An Ordinance comes into operation-

  (a)   at the beginning of the day on which it is published; or

  (b)   if provision is made for it to commence on another day, at the beginning of that other day.

(3) If an Ordinance is to commence on, or be repealed from, a day to be notified in the Gazette, the notice may fix different days for different provisions to commence or from which different provisions are to be repealed and different notices may fix different days for different provisions.

Disallowance

21.(1) Where any Ordinance is disallowed by Her Majesty, such disallowance shall be notified by the Governor by notice in the Gazette; and from and after the date of publication of such notice the Ordinance shall cease to have effect.

(2) Where notice of disallowance of any Ordinance is notified in accordance with the provisions of subsection (1), the provisions of section 23 shall apply in respect of such disallowance as if the words "disallowance" and "disallowed" were substituted therein for the words "repeal" and "repealed" respectively.

(3) Any Ordinance repealed or amended by any Ordinance disallowed shall revive and continue in force in its original form with effect from the date of publication of the notice referred to in subsection (1).

22.   (*Repealed*)

Effect of repeal generally

23.   Where an Ordinance repeals in whole or in part any other Ordinance, the repeal shall not-

  (a)   revive anything not in force or existing at the time at which the repeal takes effect;

  (b)   affect the previous operation of any Ordinance so repealed or anything duly done or suffered under any Ordinance so repealed;

(c)   affect any right, privilege, obligation or liability acquired, accrued or incurred under any Ordinance so repealed;

(d)   affect any penalty, forfeiture or punishment incurred in respect of any offence committed against any Ordinance so repealed; or

(e)   affect any investigation, legal proceeding or remedy in respect of any such right, privilege, obligation, liability, penalty, forfeiture or punishment as aforesaid; and any such investigation, legal proceeding or remedy may be instituted, continued or enforced, and any such penalty, forfeiture or punishment may be imposed, as if the repealing Ordinance had not been passed.

Repealed Ordinance not revived

24. Where any Ordinance repealing in whole or in part any former Ordinance is itself repealed, such last repeal shall not revive the Ordinance or provision previously repealed, unless provision is made to that effect.

Repeal and substitution

25. Where any Ordinance repeals in whole or in part any other Ordinance and substitutes other provisions therefor, the repealed Ordinance shall remain in force until the substituted provisions come into operation.

26. *(Repealed)*

Effect of expiry of Ordinance

27. Upon the expiry or lapse of any Ordinance, the provisions of section 23 shall apply as if such Ordinance had been repealed.

PART V - Subsidiary Legislation

General provision with regard to power to make subsidiary legislation

28.(1) Where an Ordinance confers power on a person to make subsidiary legislation, the following provisions shall have effect with reference to the subsidiary legislation-

(a) when any subsidiary legislation purports to be made in exercise of a particular power or powers, it shall be deemed also to be made in exercise of all other powers that enable its making;

(b) no subsidiary legislation shall be inconsistent with the provisions of any Ordinance;

(c) subsidiary legislation may at any time be amended by the same person and in the same manner by and in which it was made;

(ca) where the person referred to in paragraph (c) has been replaced wholly or in part by another person, the power conferred by paragraph (c) may be exercised by the other person for all matters in his jurisdiction as if he were the original person;

(d) where any Ordinance confers power on any person to make subsidiary legislation for any general purpose, and also for any incidental special purpose, the enumeration of the special purposes shall not be deemed to derogate from the generality of the powers conferred with reference to the general purpose;

(e) subsidiary legislation may provide that a contravention or breach of the subsidiary legislation is an offence punishable on summary conviction by such fine not exceeding $5,000 or by such term of imprisonment not exceeding 6 months as may be specified in the subsidiary legislation or by both such fine and imprisonment;

(f) subsidiary legislation may amend any forms contained in the Ordinance under which such subsidiary legislation is made and may prescribe new forms.

(g) *(Repealed)*

(2) Subsidiary legislation shall be published in the Gazette.

(3) Subsidiary legislation comes into operation-

    (a)   at the beginning of the day on which it is published; or

    (b)   if provision is made for it to commence on another day, at the beginning of that other day.

(4) A person who makes subsidiary legislation may provide for the subsidiary legislation to commence on a day to be fixed by notice to be given by him or by some other person designated in the subsidiary legislation.

(5) If subsidiary legislation is to commence on, or be repealed from, a day to be notified in the Gazette, the notice may fix different days for different provisions to commence or from which different provisions are to be repealed and different notices may fix different days for different provisions.

Fees and charges

29.(1A) Where an Ordinance confers a power on a person to make subsidiary legislation, the subsidiary legislation may impose a fee or charge for any thing in it or the ordinance.

(1) Where provision is made by any subsidiary legislation in respect of fees or other charges, such subsidiary legislation may provide for all or any of the following matters-

    (a)   specific fees or charges;

    (b)   maximum or minimum fees or charges;

    (c)   maximum and minimum fees or charges;

    (d)   the payment of fees or charges either generally or under specified conditions or in specified circumstances;

    (e)   the exemption of any person or class of persons from the payment of fees or charges; and

    (f)   the reduction, waiver or refund, in whole or in part, of any such fees or charges, either upon the happening of a certain event or in the discretion of a specified person.

(2) Where any reduction, waiver or refund, in whole or in part, of any fee or charge is provided for by any subsidiary legislation, such reduction, waiver or refund may be expressed to apply or be applicable either generally or specially-

(a)   in respect of certain matters or transactions or classes of matters or transactions;

(b)   in respect of certain documents or classes of documents;

(c)   in respect of the occurrence or the termination of any event;

(d)   in respect of certain persons or classes of persons; or

(e)   in respect of any combination of such matters, transactions, documents, events or persons,

and may be expressed to apply or be applicable subject to such conditions as may be specified in the subsidiary legislation or in the discretion of any person specified therein.

Variation of certain fees and charges

29A.(1) Where the amount of any fee or charge is for the time being specified in, or otherwise fixed or determined by, subsidiary legislation made by the Governor in Council, subject to subsection (2), the Financial Secretary may by similar subsidiary legislation increase or decrease, or otherwise vary, the amount of the fee or charge.

(2)   (a)   The Governor in Council may by a direction in writing direct the Financial Secretary to exercise, as regards fees or charges specified in the direction, a power conferred on him by subsection (1) either-

          (i)   only with the prior approval of the Governor in Council; or

          (ii)   so as not to exceed limits specified in the direction; or

          (iii)   only in some other manner so specified.

      (b)   For so long as a direction under this subsection is in force the Financial Secretary shall comply with it.

(3) The powers conferred by subsection (1) are in addition to, and are not in substitution for, any power exercisable by the Governor in Council in relation to fees or charges.

(4) Where-

      (a)   a power under subsection (1) is exercisable; and

      (b)   the subsidiary legislation by which the relevant fee or charge was specified, fixed or otherwise determined ("the primary instrument") is-

    (i)   subsidiary legislation to which section 35 applies or to which section 34 does not apply; or

    (ii)   subsidiary legislation of which a draft was required to be laid on the table of the Legislative Council,

then such 1 or more of the following provisions as are appropriate in the particular circumstances shall operate-

    (i)   section 35 shall apply to subsidiary legislation made or issued in exercise of the power which amends the primary instrument;

    (ii)   section 34 shall not apply to such subsidiary legislation;

    (iii)   the enactment requiring or otherwise relevant to so laying the primary instrument shall also apply to subsidiary legislation which is so made or issued and amends that instrument.

30.   (*Repealed*)

Construction of subsidiary legislation

31.(1) Where any Ordinance confers power to make any subsidiary legislation, expressions used in the subsidiary legislation shall have the same meaning as in the Ordinance conferring the power, and any reference in such subsidiary legislation to "the Ordinance" shall be construed as a reference to the Ordinance conferring the power to make such subsidiary legislation.

(2) Where in subsidiary legislation there is a reference to a section or other provision by number, letter or combination of number and letter, and not in conjunction with the title or short title of other subsidiary legislation or an Ordinance, the reference shall be construed as a reference to the section or other provision of that number, letter or combination in the subsidiary legislation in which the reference occurs.

(3) Where in subsidiary legislation there is a reference to a subsection or other subdivision of a provision by number, letter or combination of number and letter, and not in conjunction with the number of any other section or provision of that subsidiary legislation or any other subsidiary legislation, the reference shall be construed as a reference to the subsection or other subdivision of a provision of that number, letter or combination in the section or other provision in which the reference occurs.

Exercise of statutory powers between enactment and commencement of Ordinance

32.(1) Where an Ordinance is to come into operation on a day other than the day of its publication in the Gazette, a power to do anything under the Ordinance may be exercised at any time after its publication in the Gazette.

(2) An exercise of a power under subsection (1) is not effective until the provision in the Ordinance to which it relates comes into operation unless the exercise of the power is necessary to bring the Ordinance into operation.

33. *(Repealed)*

Placing of subsidiary legislation before Legislative Council

34.(1) All subsidiary legislation shall be laid on the table of the Legislative Council at the next sitting thereof after the publication in the Gazette of that subsidiary legislation.

(2) Where subsidiary legislation has been laid on the table of the Legislative Council under subsection (1), the Legislative Council may, by resolution passed at a sitting of the Legislative Council held not later than 28 days after the sitting at which it was so laid, provide that such subsidiary legislation shall be amended in any manner whatsoever consistent with the power to make such subsidiary legislation, and if any such resolution is so passed the subsidiary legislation shall, without prejudice to anything done thereunder, be deemed to be amended as from the date of publication in the Gazette of such resolution.

(3)   If the period referred to in subsection (2) would but for this subsection expire-

> *(a)*   after the last sitting before the end of a session or dissolution of the Legislative Council; but

> *(b)*   on or before the day of the second sitting of the Legislative Council in the next session,

that period shall be deemed to extend to and expire on the day after that second sitting.

(4) Before the expiry of the period referred to in subsection (2) or that period as extended by virtue of subsection (3), the Legislative Council may by resolution in relation to any subsidiary legislation specified therein extend that period or that period as so extended to the next sitting.

(5) Any resolution passed by the Legislative Council in accordance with this section shall be published in the Gazette not later than 14 days after the passing thereof or within such further period as the Governor may allow in any particular case.

(6) In this section-

"sitting", when used to calculate time, means the day on which the sitting commences and only includes a sitting at which subsidiary legislation is included on the order paper;

"subsidiary legislation" does not include a resolution of the Legislative Council.

Approval of Legislative Council to subsidiary legislation

35. Where any Ordinance provides that subsidiary legislation shall be subject to the approval of the Legislative Council or of any other authority, or contains words to the like effect, then-

   (a)   the subsidiary legislation shall be submitted for the approval of the Legislative Council or other authority; and

   (b)   the Legislative Council may by resolution or the other authority may by order amend the whole or any part of the subsidiary legislation.

Effect of repeal on subsidiary legislation

36.(1) Where any Ordinance

   (a)   repeals any former Ordinance and substitutes other provisions therefor; or

   (b)   repeals any former Ordinance and re-enacts such former Ordinance with or without modification,

any subsidiary legislation made under the former Ordinance and in force at the commencement of the repealing Ordinance shall, so far as it is not inconsistentwith the repealing Ordinance, continue in force and have the like effect for allpurposes as if made under the repealing Ordinance.

(2) Where any subsidiary legislation is continued in force by virtue ofsubsection (1), such subsidiary legislation may be from time to time amended asif it had been made under the repealing Ordinance.

Forms

37.(1) Where any form is prescribed by or under any Ordinance, deviations therefrom, not affecting the substance of such form, shall not invalidate it.

(2)   Where a form is prescribed in any Ordinance in both official languages and the text in one official language is combined in a particular manner with, or is set out separately from, the text in the other official language, the form may be printed and used-

   (a)   with the texts combined in any manner; or

   (b)   in either official language.

PART VI - Powers

Presumption of lawful exercise of power

38. Where any Ordinance confers power upon any person to-

(a)   make any subsidiary legislation;

(b)   make any instrument; or

(c)   exercise any power,

and the Ordinance conferring the power prescribes conditions, subject to the observance, performance or existence of which any such power may be exercised, such conditions shall be presumed to have been duly fulfilled if in the subsidiary legislation, the instrument or the document evidencing the exercise of the power there is a statement that the subsidiary legislation or instrument is made, or the power exercised, in exercise of, or in pursuance of, the power conferred by such Ordinance, or a statement to the like effect.

Exercise of powers

39.(1) Where any Ordinance confers any power or imposes any duty, then the power may be exercised and the duty shall be performed from time to time as occasion requires.

(2) Where any Ordinance confers any power or imposes any duty on the holder of any public office as such, then the power may be exercised and the duty shall be performed by the holder for the time being of that public office.

Construction of enabling words

40.(1) Where any Ordinance confers upon any person power to do or enforce the doing of any act or thing, all such powers shall be deemed to be also conferred as are reasonably necessary to enable the person to do or enforce the doing of the act or thing.

(2)   Without prejudice to the generality of subsection (1), where any Ordinance confers power-

(a)   to provide for, prohibit, control or regulate any matter, such power shall include power to provide for the same by the licensing thereof and power to prohibit acts whereby the prohibition, control or regulation of such matter might be evaded;

(b)   to grant a licence, Crown lease, permit, authority, approval or exemption, such power shall include power to impose reasonable conditions subject to which such licence, Crown lease, permit, authority, approval or exemption may be granted;

(c)   to approve any person or thing, such power shall include power to withdraw approval thereof,

(d)   to give directions, such power shall include power to couch the same in the form of prohibitions.

(3)-(4) *(Repealed)*

Power to issue licences, etc. discretionary

41.(1) Where any Ordinance confers power upon any person to issue, grant, give or renew any licence, Crown lease, authority, approval, exemption or permit, the person so empowered shall have a discretion either to issue, grant, give or renew or to refuse to issue, grant, give or renew such licence, Crown lease, authority, approval, exemption or permit.

(2) Nothing in this section shall affect any right which may be conferred by any Ordinance upon any person to appeal against a refusal to issue, grant, give or renew any licence, Crown lease, authority, approval, exemption or permit.

Power to appoint includes power to suspend, dismiss, re-appoint, etc.

42. Where any Ordinance confers a power or imposes a duty upon any person to make any appointment or to constitute or establish any board, tribunal, commission, committee or similar body, then the person having such power or duty shall also have the power-

(a)   to remove, suspend, dismiss or revoke the appointment of, and to re-appoint or reinstate, any person appointed in exercise of such power or duty;

(b)   to revoke the appointment, constitution or establishment of, or to dissolve, any board, tribunal, commission, committee or similar body appointed, constituted or established, in exercise of such power or duty, and to re-appoint, re-constitute or re-establish the same; and

(c)   to specify the period for which any person appointed in exercise of such power or duty shall hold such appointment:

Provided that where the power or duty of such person so to act is only exercisable upon the recommendation, or is subject to the approval or consent, of some other person, then such power shall only be exercisable upon such recommendation or subject to such approval or consent.

Delegation by specified public officers

43.(1) Where any Ordinance confers powers or imposes duties upon a specified public officer, such public officer may delegate any other public officer or the person for the time being holding any office designated by him to exercise such powers or perform such duties on his behalf, and thereupon, or from the date specified by such specified public officer, the person delegated shall have and may exercise such powers and perform such duties.

(2) Nothing in subsection (1) shall authorize a specified public officer todelegate any person to make subsidiary legislation or to hear any appeal.

(3) Where any Ordinance confers any power or imposes any duty upon a specified public officer and such power is exercised or such duty is performed by any other public officer, the specified public officer shall, unless the contrary is proved, be deemed to have delegated the latter public officer under subsection (1) to exercise the power or perform the duty.

(4) In this section "specified public officer" means the person for the time being holding any public office which has been specified, either generally or for the purposes of any particular Ordinance, under this section by the Governor by notice in the Gazette.

Effect of delegation of powers and duties

44.(1) Where any Ordinance confers power upon any person to delegate the exercise on his behalf of any of the powers or the performance of any of the duties conferred or imposed upon him under any Ordinance-

    (a)   such delegation shall not preclude the person so delegating from exercising or performing at any time any of the powers or duties so delegated;

    (b)   such delegation may be conditional, qualified or limited in such manner as the person so delegating may think fit;

    (c)   where the delegation may be made only with the approval of some person, such delegation may be conditional, qualified or limited in such manner as the person whose approval is required may think fit;

    (d)   the delegation may be to a named person or to the person for the time being holding any office designated by the person so delegating; and

    (e)   any delegation may be amended by the person so delegating.

(2) The delegation of any power shall be deemed to include the delegation of any duty incidental thereto or connected therewith and the delegation of any duty shall be deemed to include the delegation of any power incidental thereto or connected therewith.

Exercise of powers in special cases

45. Where any Ordinance confers any power or imposes any duty upon theholder of any public office and either-

    (a)   that office has been abolished; or

    (b)   no person has been appointed to discharge the functions of that office,

those powers and duties may be exercised or performed-

    (i)   in the case of making subsidiary legislation, by the Governor; and

    (ii)   in any other case, by the holder of such other public office as the Governor may by order direct.

Power to make public instruments and perform acts

46. Where any Ordinance confers power upon any person to make, grant, issue or approve any proclamation, order, notice, declaration, instrument, notification, licence, permit, exemption, register or list, such power shall include power-

    (a)   to amend or suspend such proclamation, order, notice, declaration, instrument, notification, licence, permit, exemption, register or list;

    (b)   to substitute another proclamation, order, notice, declaration, instrument, notification, licence, permit, exemption, register or list for one already made, granted, issued or approved;

    (c)   to withdraw approval of any proclamation, order, notice, declaration, instrument, notification, licence, permit, exemption, register or list so approved; and

    (d)   to declare the date of the coming into operation, and the period of operation, of any such proclamation, order, notice, declaration, instrument, notification, licence, permit, exemption, register or list.

Power to relate back appointment

47. Any appointment made under the provisions of any Ordinance may be declared to have effect as from the date upon which the person appointed in fact began to exercise the powers and perform the duties of his appointment, not being a date earlier than the commencement of the Ordinance under which the appointment is made.

PART VII - Boards and Committees

Power of Governor to appoint advisory bodies

47A.(1) The Governor may from time to time by order published in the Gazette establish by law such advisory and other committees and bodies as he considers appropriate in the public interest and may appoint the members thereof.

(2) An order under subsection (1) may contain such provisions relating to the committee or body established by the order as the Governor thinks fit, including the terms of reference of the body, the terms of office of members appointed to that body, the removal or resignation of members, the re-appointment of members, quorums for meetings and similar procedural matters.

Power to appoint chairman

48. Where any Ordinance confers power upon any person to appoint any persons to be members of any board, tribunal, commission, committee or similar body, the person so appointing may appoint a chairman, a deputy chairman, a vice-chairman and a secretary of such board, tribunal, commission, committee or similar body.

Power to appoint public officer to board, etc.

49. Where any Ordinance confers power upon any person to appoint any persons to be members of any board, tribunal, commission, committee or similar body, the person so empowered may appoint any public officer, by his official designation, to be a member of such board, tribunal, commission, committee or similar body, and, on such appointment and until such appointment shall be revoked or otherwise determined, the person for the time being holding the public office in question shall be a member of such board, tribunal, commission, committee or similar body.

Appointment of alternates

50. Where any board, tribunal, commission, committee or similar body is established by or under any Ordinance, any person who is empowered by such Ordinance to appoint any or all of the members thereof may-

> *(a)* appoint 1 or more duly qualified persons to be alternate members of the same, and any one such alternate member may attend any meeting of the same when a substantive member is temporarily unable to attend for any reason; and

> *(b)* appoint a duly qualified person to be a temporary member of the same in the place of any substantive member who is precluded by illness, absence from the Colony or any other cause from exercising his functions as such,

and when attending any meeting of such board, tribunal, commission, committee or similar body, such alternate or temporary member shall be deemed for all purposes to be a member of the same.

Powers of board, etc. not affected by vacancy

51. Where any board, tribunal, commission, committee or similar body is established by or under any Ordinance, the powers of such board, tribunal, commission, committee or similar body shall not be affected by-

> *(a)* any vacancy in the membership thereof;

> *(b)* any defect in the appointment or qualification of a person purporting to be a member thereof; or

> *(c)* any minor irregularity in the convening of any meeting thereof.

Power of majority and exercise of powers

52.(1) Where any Ordinance confers a power or imposes a duty upon a body or number of persons consisting of or being not less than 3, such power may be exercised or duty performed in the name of that body or number of persons by a majority of those persons.

(2) Whenever such body or number of persons is assembled, the chairman or other member presiding shall have a casting as well as a deliberative vote, in all matters in which a decision is taken by vote by whatever name such vote may be called.

(3) The exercise of any power vested in such body or number of persons may be signified either by the chairman or other person presiding at the meeting or other deliberation at which such power was exercised or at which, as the case may be, authority to exercise it was conferred, or by any person from time to time authorized by such body or persons to signify the exercise of such power.

Seal

53. Where any Ordinance constitutes any board, tribunal, commission, committee or similar body to be a body corporate having perpetual succession and a common seal, and any document requires to be sealed with such common seal, then such common seal shall be affixed by the chairman of such board, tribunal, commission, committee or similar body, or by any member thereof appointed by the chairman for that purpose, and shall be authenticated by the signature of the chairman or such member.

PART VIII - Public Officers and Public Contracts

References to public officer

54. In any Ordinance, instrument, warrant or process of any kind, any reference to a public officer, or to a person holding a public office by a term designating his office, shall include a reference to any person for the time being lawfully discharging the functions of that office, or any part of such functions, and any person appointed to act in or perform the duties of such office, or any part of such duties, for the time being.

Power to transfer functions of public officers

54A.(1) The Legislative Council may by resolution provide for the transfer to any public officer of any functions exercisable by virtue of any Ordinance by another public officer.

(2) A resolution under this section may contain such incidental, consequential and supplemental provisions as may be necessary or expedient for the purpose of giving full effect to the resolution.

(3) A certificate issued by the Chief Secretary that any property vested in a public officer immediately before a resolution under this section takes effect has been transferred by virtue of the resolution to another public officer shall be conclusive evidence of the transfer.

(4) In this section-

"functions" includes powers and duties;

"public officer" includes any corporation created for the purpose of incorporating a person for the time being holding a public office.

Change of title of office

55. The Chief Secretary may, by notice (which may be given retrospective effect) in the Gazette, declare a change in title of any public officer or public body, or of any person referred to in any Ordinance, and the notice may contain provisions substituting the new title in any Ordinance relating to the public officer, public body or person and in any instrument, contract or legal proceedings made or commenced before the date on which the notice takes effect.

Appointment of officers by name or office

56. Where any Ordinance confers power upon any person to appoint or name a person to have and exercise any powers or perform any duties, the person so empowered may either appoint a person by name or direct the person for the time being holding any office designated by him to have and exercise such powers or perform such duties; and thereupon, or from the date specified by the person so empowered, the person appointed by name or the person holding the office aforesaid shall have and may exercise such powers or perform such duties accordingly until such appointment be revoked or otherwise determined.

Filling vacancy

57.(1) When any Ordinance confers a power or imposes a duty upon a public officer and such public officer is unable to exercise the powers or perform the duties of his office, owing to absence or inability to act from illness or any other cause, the Governor may, by notice in the Gazette, direct that such power shall be had and may be exercised and such duty shall be performed by a public officer named by, or by a public officer holding the office designated by, the Governor, subject to such conditions, exceptions and qualifications as the Governor may direct.

(2) Any direction by the Governor under subsection (1) may be given-

> *(a)*   in anticipation of any absence or inability occurring; or

> *(b)*   subsequently thereto and may relate back to the commencement of such absence or inability.

(3) Where any Ordinance confers powers or imposes duties upon a public officer and a new post is subsequently created in the same or another Government department, the Governor may, by notice in the Gazette, direct that the said powers and duties or any of them shall be exercised by any holder of the new post so created, either to the exclusion of or in addition to the first named public officer or otherwise.

Power to appoint while holder on retirement leave

58.(1) Where the holder of any public office is on leave of absence pending the relinquishment by him of such office, another person may be appointed to the same public office.

(2) Where 2 or more persons are holding the same public office by reason of an appointment made in accordance with subsection (1), then, for the purposes of any Ordinance and in respect of any power conferred or duty imposed upon the holder of such office, the person last appointed to the office shall be deemed to be the holder thereof.

Contracts by public officer

59. In any contract or other document, signed, executed or made by the Governor or by any public officer on behalf of the Governor or the Government or of any Government department, it shall not be necessary to name the Governor or such public officer, but it shall be sufficient to name the office held by the Governor or such public officer, and the Governor or public officer shall be deemed to be a party thereto as if the Governor or such public officer were a corporation sole with perpetual succession for this purpose.

Effect of past contracts by public officer

60. Any contract or other document signed, executed or made before the commencement of this Ordinance by the Governor or by any public officer on behalf of the Governor or the Government or of any Government department shall be enforceable as if the office of Governor or such public officer had, at the time of such execution or making, been a corporation sole with perpetual succession for this purpose.

Omission of title after signature of public officer immaterial

61. The omission to add the title of the public office held by the Governor or any public officer signing or executing any contract or other document after the signature of such officer shall not exclude such contract or other document from the operation of sections 59 and 60.

PART IX - Crown, Governor and Governor in Council

Signification of orders of Governor and Governor in Council

62.(1) Where any Ordinance confers a power or imposes a duty upon the Governor or the Governor in Council to make any subsidiary legislation or appointment, give any directions, issue any order, authorize any thing or matter to be done, grant any exemption, remit any fee or penalty, or exercise any other power or perform any other duty, the exercise of such power or the performance of such duty may be signified-

> *(a)*   in the case of the Governor, under the hand of any public officer specified in Schedule 6;

> *(b)*   in the case of the Governor in Council, under the hand of the Clerk to the Executive Council.

(2) Notwithstanding the provisions of subsection (1), proclamations shall be made or issued only under the hand of the Governor himself.

(3) The Governor may, by order published in the Gazette, amend Schedule 6.

Delegation by Governor

63.(1) Where any Ordinance confers powers or imposes duties upon the Governor, he may delegate any person by name or the person holding any office designated by him to exercise such powers or perform such duties on his behalf and thereupon, or from the date specified by the Governor, the person so delegated shall have and may exercise such powers and perform such duties.

(2) Without prejudice to the provisions of any Letters Patent or Royal Instructions relating to the appointment of a deputy to the Governor, nothing in subsection (1) shall authorize the Governor to delegate any person to make subsidiary legislation, issue proclamations or to determine any appeal.

(3) Where any Ordinance confers powers or imposes duties upon the Governor and such power is exercised or such duty is performed by any public officer, the Governor shall, unless the contrary is proved, be deemed to have delegated such public officer under subsection (1) to exercise the power or perform the duty.

Appeals and objections to Governor in Council

64.(1) Where any Ordinance confers upon any person a right of appeal or objection to the Governor in Council, such appeal or objection shall be governed by rules made in accordance with subsection (2).

(2) The Governor in Council may make rules governing the procedure to be followed in appeals or objections to the Governor in Council.

(3) The conferring by any Ordinance of a right of appeal or objection to the Governor in Council shall not prevent any person from applying to the Supreme Court for an order of mandamus, certiorari, prohibition, injunction or any other order, instead of appealing or making an objection to the Governor in Council, where an application for such an order would lie, but no proceedings by way of mandamus, certiorari, prohibition, injunction or other order shall be taken against the Governor in Council in respect of any such appeal or objection to the Governor in Council or any proceedings connected therewith.

(4) The Governor in Council, when considering any appeal or objection to him (whether by way of petition or otherwise, and whether such appeal or objection is made by virtue of any Ordinance or otherwise) shall act in an administrative or executive capacity and not in a judicial or quasi-judicial capacity and shall be entitled to consider and take into account any evidence, material, information or advice in his absolute discretion.

(5) The Governor in Council, when considering any appeal or objection to him (whether by way of petition or otherwise and whether such appeal or objection is made by virtue of any Ordinance or otherwise) against any decision of any person, public officer or public body, may confirm, vary or reverse such decision or substitute therefor such other decision or make such other order as the Governor in Council may think fit.

References to the Sovereign

65. Any reference to the Sovereign or to the Crown shall be construed as a reference to the Sovereign for the time being.

Saving of rights of Crown

66. No Ordinance shall in any manner whatsoever affect the right of or be binding on the Crown unless it is therein expressly provided or unless it appears by necessary implication that the Crown is bound thereby.

PART X - Time and Distance

Hong Kong Time

67.(1) Whenever any expression of time occurs in any Ordinance the time referred to is Hong Kong Time.

(2) For the purposes of subsection (1), "Hong Kong Time" means the time used for general purposes throughout Hong Kong namely, 8 hours, or such other period as may be determined by the Legislative Council by resolution under this subsection or under section 16 of the Oil (Conservation and Control) Ordinance (Cap. 264), in advance of Greenwich Mean Time.

(3) A resolution of the Legislative Council under subsection (2) may determine Hong Kong Time for the whole or part of a year.

(4) Nothing in this section shall affect the use of Greenwich Mean Time for the purposes of astronomy, meteorology, navigation or aviation, or affect the construction of any document mentioning or referring to a point of time in connection with any of these purposes.

68. *(Repealed)*

References to "a.m." and "p.m."

69. The expression "a.m." indicates the period between midnight and the following noon, and the expression "p.m." indicates the time between noon and the following midnight. Where 2 such expressions occur conjunctively in relation to any specified hour or in conjunction with the word "sunset" or "sunrise", they shall be construed as relating to a consecutive period of time.

Provision where no time prescribed

70. Where no time is prescribed or allowed within which any thing shall be done, such thing shall be done without unreasonable delay, and as often as due occasion arises.

Computation of time

71.(1) In computing time for the purposes of any Ordinance-

    (a)   a period of days from the happening of any event or the doing of any act or thing shall be deemed to be exclusive of the day on which the event happens or the act or thing is done;

(b)   if the last day of the period is a public holiday or a gale warning day the period shall include the next following day, not being a public holiday or a gale warning day;

(c)   where any act or proceeding is directed or allowed to be done or taken on a certain day, then if that day is a public holiday or a gale warning day, the act or proceeding shall be considered as done or taken in due time if it is done or taken on the next following day, not being a public holiday or a gale warning day;

(d)   where an act or proceeding is directed or allowed to be done or taken within any time not exceeding 6 days, no public holiday or a gale warning day shall be reckoned in the computation of that time.

(2) In this section "gale warning day" means any day throughout or for part of which a gale warning is in force, and "gale warning" has the meaning assigned to it by section 2 of the Judicial Proceedings (Adjournment During Gale Warnings) Ordinance (Cap. 62).

Power to extend time

72. Where in any Ordinance a time is prescribed for doing any act or taking any proceeding and power is given to a court, public body, public officer or other authority to extend such time, then the power may be exercised by the court, public body, public officer or other authority although the application for the same is not made until after the expiration of the time prescribed.

Distance

73. In the measurement of any distance for the purposes of any Ordinance, that distance shall be measured in a straight line on a horizontal plane.

Warrants, etc. valid on public holiday

74. Any summons, notice, warrant or other process may be issued, served or executed and any arrest, search or seizure may be carried out or made on any day, whether a public holiday or not, and at any hour of the day or night.

PART XI - Imperial Enactments

Modifications

75. An imperial enactment shall be judicially noticed as such and shall be read with such modifications as to names, localities, courts, officers, persons, moneys, penalties or otherwise as may be necessary to make the same applicable to the circumstances of the Colony.

Citation of imperial enactments

76. An imperial enactment may be cited by a short title or citation, if any, or by reference to the regnal or calendar year in which it was passed or by the number assigned to any statutory instrument or statutory rule and order.

Construction of reference to imperial enactment

77. A reference in any law to an imperial enactment or to any provision, part or division thereof shall be construed as a reference to the same as the same may be from time to time amended on or before 1 January 1994 and as a reference to any imperial enactment or to any provision, part or division of an imperial enactment, substituted for it on or before 1 January 1994.

References to subsidiary legislation under imperial Acts

78. A reference in any law to any imperial Act shall include a reference to any Order in Council, rule, regulation, proclamation, order, notice, rule of court, by-law or other instrument made under or by virtue thereof and having legislative effect.

79. (*Repealed*)

Copies of imperial enactments

80. A copy of an imperial enactment shall, if it-

> (a) is published in the Gazette or purports to be printed by the Government Printer; or

> (b) is contained in any printed collection purporting to be published or printed by authority,

be deemed, until the contrary is proved, to be an authentic copy of the imperial enactment as at the date of such publication or printing.

PART XII

(Repealed)

PART XIII - Miscellaneous

Copies of Ordinances, etc. in Gazette

98.(1) A copy of an Ordinance shall, if published in the Gazette, be deemed to be an authentic copy of that Ordinance as at the date of such publication.

(2) A copy of any other instrument shall, if published in the Gazette or purporting to be printed by the Government Printer, on its production be admitted as prima facie evidence thereof in all courts and for all purposes whatsoever without any further proof.

Rectification of errors

98A.(1) The Attorney General may, by order published in the Gazette, rectify any clerical or printing error appearing in any Ordinance printed or published pursuant to this Ordinance.

(2) Every order made under this section shall be laid on the table of the Legislative Council without unreasonable delay, and, if a resolution is passed at the first sitting of the Legislative Council held not less than 27 days after the sitting at which the order is so laid that the order be annulled, it shall thenceforth be void, but without prejudice to the validity of anything previously done thereunder, or to the making of a new order.

(3) In this section, "sitting", when used to calculate time, means the day on which the sitting commences and only includes a sitting at which subsidiary legislation is included on the order paper.

Reprint of Ordinances

99. The Government Printer may, with the authority of the Governor, print copies of any Ordinance with all additions, omissions, substitutions and amendments effected by any amending Ordinances, and such copies shall be deemed to be authentic copies of the Ordinance so amended as at the date of such printing.

100. *(Repealed)*

Power to increase fines

100A.(1) The Legislative Council may, by resolution, amend an Ordinance so as to increase-

(a)   the amount of a fine specified in the Ordinance; and

(b)   the amount of a fine specified in the Ordinance as an amount that may be prescribed in subsidiary legislation made under the Ordinance.

(1A)   The increase under subsection (1) may be expressed as an amount of money or as a level in Schedule 8 to the Criminal Procedure Ordinance (Cap.221).

(2) A resolution under this section may contain such incidental, consequential and supplemental provisions as may be necessary or expedient for the purpose of giving full effect to the resolution.

Amendment of Schedules

101. The Governor may from time to time, by notice in the Gazette, amend all or any of the Schedules.

SCHEDULE 1

Boundaries of The City of Victoria

On the north -The Harbour;

On the west - A line running due north and south drawn through the north-west angle of Inland Lot No. 1299 and extending southwards a distance of 850 feet from the aforesaid angle; On the south-A line running due east from the southern extremity of the western boundary until it meets a contour in the vicinity of the Hill above Belchers 700 feet above principal datum, that is to say, a level 17.833 feet below the bench-mark known as "Rifleman's Bolt", the highest point of a copper bolt set horizontally in the east wall of the Royal Navy Office and Mess Block Naval Dockyard, and thence following the said contour until it meets the eastern boundary; On the east-A line following the west side of the Government Pier, Bay View and thence along the west side of Hing Fat Street, then along the north side of Causeway Road to Moreton Terrace. Thence along the west side of Moreton Terrace to the south-east corner of Inland Lot No. 1580 and produced in a straight line for 80 feet, and thence along the north side of Cotton Path and produced until it meets the west side of Wong Nei Chong Road on the east side of Wong Nei Chong Valley and thence to the south-east angle of Inland Lot No. 1364, produced until it meets the southern boundary.

SCHEDULE 2

Boundaries of The Colony

On the south - The parallel of latitude 22°09' north between the points where it is intersected by the meridian of longitude 114°30' east of Greenwich and the line of the western boundary; On the north-A line drawn from the point where the meridian of longitude 113°52' east of Greenwich intersects the parallel of latitude touching the extreme south-west point of the shore of Deep Bay to the said south-west point of the shore of Deep Bay; thence along the high water mark upon the shore of Deep Bay to the estuary of the Sham Chun River; thence by a line drawn as described in the agreement delineating the northern frontier of the New Territories signed by James Haldane Steward LOCKHART and WONG Tsun-shin at Hong Kong on 19 March 1899, and following the high water mark in Mirs Bay to the point where the meridian of longitude 114°30' east of Greenwich intersects the mainland high water mark; On the east-The meridian of longitude 114°30' east of Greenwich between the points where it intersects the mainland high water mark and the parallel of latitude 22°09' north; On the west-The meridian of longitude 113°52' east of Greenwich between the point where it intersects the parallel of latitude touching the extreme south-west point of the shore of Deep Bay and the north coast of Lantau Island. The boundary then follows the western coast line of Lantau Island including the waters appertaining thereto to the extreme south-west point thereof and thence runs in a south-easterly direction to the extreme south-west point of Tai A Chau Island in the Soko Island Group and continues in the same straight line to the point at which it intersects the parallel of latitude 22°09' north.

SCHEDULE 3

Boundaries of The Harbour

On the east - A straight line drawn from the westernmost extremity of Siu Chau Wan Point to the westernmost extremity of Ah Kung Ngam Point (sometimes known as Kung Am); On the west-A straight line drawn from the westernmost point of Island of Hong Kong to the westernmost point of Green Island, thence a straight line drawn from the westernmost point of Green Island to the south-easternmost point of Tsing Yi, thence along the eastern and northern coast lines of Tsing Yi to the westernmost extremity of Tsing Yi and thence a straight line drawn true north therefrom to the mainland.

SCHEDULE 4

Area of Kowloon

"Kowloon" means that portion of the peninsula of Kaulung which was ceded to Great Britain by the Emperor of China on 24 October 1860.

SCHEDULE 5

Area Of New Kowloon

"New Kowloon" means that portion of the New Territories which is delineated in red and shown upon a plan marked "New Kowloon" dated 8 December 1937, signed by the Director of Public Works, countersigned by the Governor and deposited in the Land Registry.

SCHEDULE 6

Public Officers

Chief Secretary
Financial Secretary
Attorney General
Secretary for the Civil Service
Secretary for Constitutional Affairs
Secretary for Economic Services
Secretary for Education and Manpower
Secretary for Health and Welfare
Secretary for Home Affairs
Secretary for Financial Services
Secretary for Planning, Environment and Lands
Secretary for Recreation and Culture
Secretary for Security
Secretary for Trade and Industry
Secretary for Transport
Secretary for the Treasury
Director of Administration
Secretary for Works
Director of Home Affairs
Deputy Secretary
Deputy Director of Administration
Principal Assistant Secretary
Assistant Director of Administration

Hong Kong as a Tax Haven for International Business

by

Adam Starchild

Tax havens are very much in the news, and stories about small- and medium-sized companies mushrooming overnight and multi-national giants amassing fabulous fortunes via tax haven operations are growing. They may sound like Alice in Wonderland fairy tales to most people, but to the sophisticated entrepreneur, use of foreign tax havens for such advantages is an everyday business opportunity.

The use of a foreign corporation domiciled in any one of the famous company tax havens such as Hong Kong, Panama, the Bahamas, or Bermuda (among others, can enhance the profitability of any international business.

Many European and American companies are expanding and diversifying overseas as a means of growth and as a hedge against economic ups and downs in their country of origin. By incorporating a tax haven operation to accumulate tax-free income, accomplishment of multi-national objectives is accelerated. An international trading or freight operation can be established in a tax haven to be used as a conduit for international sales activity and financing. Such operations can accumulate trade discounts, commissions, advertising allowances, etc., completely tax-free while the parent or associated company can assume tax deductions by absorbing administrative and selling costs.

Before getting into the ways in which tax haven operations are used by various types of businesses, it is of eminent importance that the distinct difference is understood between two seemingly similar terms: "tax avoidance" and "tax evasion." Tax evasion has dubious and illegal overtones: for example, a company might falsify its financial statements so as to conceal its full liability to the tax authorities — that would be tax evasion — an infraction of the law and a very serious one.

Tax avoidance, on the other hand, is a legitimate method of minimizing or negating the tax factor. In simple terms, it is utilizing "loopholes" in tax laws and exploiting them within legal perimeters. This is the cornerstone of the tax haven concept.

Certain offshore companies can defer any tax until the profits are repatriated to the investor's home country. These are generally companies actively engaged in the conduct of a local business. In most import-export or other international trade activities, such a definition is especially easy to meet. A retailer, or group of retailers, could set up their own wholesale buying opertion in a convenient tax haven, such as Hong Kong, and put all of their Asian business through it. The profits of the Hong Kong firm would accumulate tax-free, and could be invested in other foreign operations.

In addition, a great many countries offer tax holidays of 5 to 20 years for new export manufacturers or assembly operations, often including smaller companies down to as few as ten employees. A company or group of companies could easily invest some of their foreign profits in such a venture, continuing to build for tax-free profits. Such concessions often include an exemption from customs duties on raw materials and equipment.

Most developed countries do tax the current income of certain types of corporations controlled by their residents, such as leasing companies, and other financial enterprises dealing the parent company. But this concept of a controlled foreign corporation applies usually to passive or tax-haven type corporations, not to active businesses. But even for a passive business, a joint venture with foreign partners on a 50-50 basis will allow the income to accumulate tax-free since the company is not controlled by national of either country. If you are leasing equipment, consider a joint venture with your foreign partner whereby you set up a jointly owned company to receive some of the income. You will both profit by it, and have a tax-free pool of funds to invest together in other ventures. Such profits will not be taxed in the country of either partner until they are repatriated, since they are not controlled by either country's citizen.

Countries which have no income tax include Bermuda, the Bahamas, the Cayman Islands, Nevis, and the Turks & Caicos Islands. A number of countries do not tax foreign source income, including Panama and Hong Kong.

Many businessmen looking for tax haven opportunities would envy the daily opportunities open to international traders, and yet most international traders rarely use these opportunities — or even understand them. 100% tax-free dollars will grow a whole lot faster than 50% after-tax dollars.

Setting Up Your Tax Haven-Based Trading Operation

A firm I can personally give my highest recommendation to is ICS Trust (Asia) Limited, based in Hong Kong.

The handover of the former British Crown Colony of Hong Kong to China is complete, and it is now called the Hong Kong Special Administrative Region, generally abbreviated to Hong Kong S.A.R., even on official documents.

As more than one local businessman has put it, "now that the politicians and journalists are gone (from covering the handover), we can get down to *business*." This attitude is typical of Hong Kong, still a true capitalist center. In fact, many of the wealthy who left to obtain second citizenships in Canada, Australia, and elsewhere, have now returned home to continue building their fortunes.

The major advantage of Hong Kong is simply that it is a real business center, not just a tax haven. One of the consequences of that is the ability to add value to services that are provided in only skeleton form in other tax havens. The reinvoicing business is a prime example. Most tax haven jurisdictions host a number of trading companies that do nothing more than reinvoicing. But one Hong Kong firm has now developed this traditional service into a "real" business mode, with an ability to arrange local trade financing. This is a healthy step away from traditional tax havenry into a true offshore **business** center.

ICS Trust Company Limited is part of the ICS International group of companies headquartered in Hong Kong. This highly successful entrepreneurial group was started by Elizabeth L. Thomson. Elizabeth describes herself as "a lawyer by profession" (2 law degrees, a member of 4 Law Societies internationally), "an entrepreneur by choice"! She has helped innumerable people start new enterprises in many parts of the globe and is well known in Hong Kong for her work with women entrepreneurs.

With a staff of 40 at ICS, every aspect of your business is covered — from deciding to incorporate, to obtaining financing from the bank, to managing your paper work including Letters of Credit, to investing your hard earned profits! ICS is truly a "one stop shop" for entrepreneurs.

Their clients range from multinational companies for whom they run Direct Import Programs worth millions of dollars to individuals who seek tax sheltering and estate planning on an international scale. As an entrepreneurial group, they attract many entrepreneurs as clients — business people who have grown their business to a level of maturity and profits that requires expansion into Asia for many diverse reasons.

Instead of just a paper thin traditional tax haven reinvoicing company, with ICS you can develop a real business in Hong Kong. With their extensive banking contacts, ICS professionals will "shop" for the best letter of credit facilities that Hong Kong's competitive banking scene can offer, likely better facilities than you can find at home. Depending upon the client, ICS can often arrange letter of credit banking facilities for clients with either a low or zero margin deposit, usually required by the opening bank. By freeing up your collateral and capital, they provide you with more purchasing power to increase sales and gain higher profits.

Most of these reinvoicing transactions are usually effected such that they are tax free in Hong Kong. There is no withholding tax on dividends so it is often possible to engage in international trade through a HK company and obtain dividends from that company tax free.

ICS will also work with international banks and factors in Hong Kong and overseas to arrange financing, secured primarily on the strength of purchase orders from your clients. Working with banks, factories, shipping companies and freight forwarders, ICS will structure a transaction to increase the likelihood of obtaining flexible, low cost facilities.

The goods do not need to go through HK for us to use a HK vehicle to pass title. Most of their clients ship from a third country direct to their own country.

Although the traditional Hong Kong focus is on firms who trade in goods, it is also possible to use these structures in cases where services are to be provided from overseas. For example, a firm could contract out a study to a company in Hong Kong. This Hong Kong company could then sub-contract out the work to a third party firm and the profit kept in Hong Kong, tax free.

If you import goods from Asia for sale to large chains, ICS can help you expand your credit facilities and increase your domestic sales by establishing and running a Direct Import Program for you. Combined with their international trade finance capabilities, the Direct Import Program is a powerful tool for generating more profits.

The primary goal of the Direct Import Program is to maximize your profits by making your customers perceive that they are buying "direct." This is achieved by:

- setting up a subsidiary company in Hong Kong

- getting your buyers to open their L/C or orders to this subsidiary

- liaising with suppliers to ensure goods are to specification.

  The Direct Import Program works because of two powerful reasons:

- The trend in the retail industry is for buyers to "buy direct" from the Orient. Having a subsidiary in Hong Kong which receives orders or L/Cs greatly enhances this perception.

- Large retail chains often can obtain freight and insurance at significant savings because of their economies of scale. Selling FOB Asia can often result in a lower selling price for the importer but with the same profit.

ICS will set up and manage the subsidiary company for you, and prepare financing proposals for presentation to local banks. When everything is complete, goods are shipped directly from the Asian factory to the customer. The fact that you are now seen as an Asian supplier (and not the middleman) is often an important factor that clinches the deal. The added prestige of a Hong Kong office makes the customer think he or she is buying "direct" and therefore receiving the lowest price.

To get started, you should contact ICS with as much detail as possible about your business and its trading activities.

For further information, contact:

Mr. Kishore K. Sakhrani, Director
ICS Trust (Asia) Limited
8th Floor, Henley Building
Five Queen's Road, Central
Hong Kong
Telephone: +852 2854 4544
Fax: +852 2543 5555

You will be well-advised and well-serviced in the hands of this fine company.

Sources of Help for Offshore Investing

Britannia Corporate Management Limited

Another business specializing in the formation of offshore corporations and trusts is Britannia Corporate Management Limited, located in the Cayman Islands. Its president, Gary F. Oakley, is a Canadian with over 18 years of Cayman Islands residency. Britannia is licensed to manage investment holding and trading companies, real estate holding companies, patent holding companies, and insurance holding companies. It is licensed to incorporate and manage corporations registered in the Cayman Islands. As such, the firm can service as the registered office of a corporation, provide its secretary, officers and directors, or undertake any day-to-day functions that may be required. More information can be obtained by writing the following:

Britannia Corporate Management Limited
Attn: New Clients Information
P. O. Box 1968
Whitewall Estates, Grand Cayman
Cayman Islands

Britannia can be reached by fax at +1 345 949 0716, marking your fax "Attention New Clients Information.

Skye Fiduciary Services Limited

Skye Fiduciary Services Limited are among the foremost experts in offshore planning. Under the direction of its chairman Charles Cain, formerly managing director of the second merchant bank to open in the Isle of Man, Skye Fiduciary is the most experienced offshore corporate and trust management business in the jurisdiction. Although Skye offers a full range of company and trust management services, their expertise in designing novel company structures to meet the needs of foreign clients is unique.

For further information, write the following:

Skye Fiduciary Services Limited
Attn: New Clients Department
2 Water Street
Ramsey, Isle of Man 1M8 1JP
United Kingdom

Their telephone number is +44 1624 816117. Fax service is available at +44 1624 816645; marking your fax "Attention: New Clients Information".

JML Swiss Investment Counsellors

One of the leaders in Swiss financial management is JML Swiss Investment Counsellors, a firm which offers a unique style of financial management. Clients can customize and control their own portfolios and still receive comprehensive management advice from some of the world's best experts on financial matters.

Recognizing that investors have differing goals, time frames, and tolerance for risk, JML's managers work with their individual clients to help them target their unique objectives. This naturally requires continued surveillance and analysis of worldwide economic trends, political events, financial markets, currencies, and other factors which could make some investments particularly attractive and others most unfavorable. Few individuals have the time or expertise to undertake this kind of evaluation themselves.

Further information about JML can be obtained by writing the following:

JML Jurg M. Lattmann AG
Swiss Investment Counsellors
Germaniastrasse 55, Dept. 212
CH-8033 Zurich, Switzerland

Their telephone number is (41) 1 368-8233 and their fax number is (41) 1 368-8299, marking your fax "Attention Department 212".

Weber Hartmann Vrijhof & Partners

While there are many excellent Swiss investment financial managers, another one of particular note is the management firm of Weber Hartmann Vrijhof & Partners. Offering management services for the portfolios of both individuals and companies, the firm excels at providing personal attention to its clients. Weber Hartmann Vrijhof & Partners was established in 1992 by Hans Weber, Robert Vrijhof, and Adrian Hartmann. The three men have substantial experience in finance and investment. Weber managed Foreign Commerce Bank (FOCOBANK) in Switzerland for nearly 30 years as its president and CEO, Vrijhof was a former vice-president and head of FOCOBANK'S portfolio management group, and Hartmann was head of FOCOBANK'S North American subsidiary in Vancouver. Weber Hartmann Vrijhof & Partners offers specialized investment services designed to meet the individual needs of their clients.

The minimum opening portfolio to be managed by this firm is $250,000 or equivalent. The management team here normally recommends that a portion of the portfolio be invested in hard currencies other than the

U.S. dollar including the Swiss franc, French franc, German mark, and Dutch guilder. Respected for their conservative approach to portfolio management, the partners assist clients with opening a custodial account at one of the major private Swiss banks, so that all client securities are held by the bank, not the investment manager.

A large percentage of their clients are based in the United States. One of their main goals has always been to get a certain portion of their clients' wealth out of the U.S. dollar and into European hard currencies such as Swiss francs, Deutschmarks, and Dutch guilders, and then build a portfolio with a mix of bonds and shares.

For more information, you can write to the following:

Weber Hartmann Vrijhof & Partners Ltd.
Attn: New Clients Department
Zurichshstrasse 110B
CH-8134 Adilswil, Switzerland

Their telephone number is (41-1) 709-11-15 and their fax number (41-1) 709-11-13, marking your fax "Attention New Clients Department".

Dunn & Hargitt International Group

Recently, many international investors have become dissatisfied with the small annual return on Euro-dollar deposits.

This is why private and institutional investors throughout the world are looking at other areas where returns can be in the area of 20-25% a year, to help offset the high annual rates of inflation on luxury goods.

The Dunn & Hargitt International Group, founded in 1961, has specialized in doing research for developing Portfolio Management Programs that have the potential of providing investors with a high return on their capital by investing in a diversified portfolio trading in the commodity, currency, precious metals, and financial futures markets in the United States and throughout the world.

The Dunn & Hargitt group offers investors the possibilitiy of participating in several of the different pools that are managed by them by investing through the investment programs that are offered by their affiliate, Winchester Life in Gibraltar, but which are actually managed by The Dunn & Hargitt International Group.

At the time of publication they are offering three possible investment alternatives, including The Winchester Life Umbrella Account (which allows 100% of a client's money to be invested in a diversified futures portfolio), The Winchester Life 100% Guaranteed Investment Account (in which Lloyds Bank acts as custodian trustee and US Government Zero Coupon Treasury Bonds are set aside to guarantee the client's capital), and The Winchester Life 150% Guaranteed Investment Account (which is a similar program, but guaranteeing that the client will receive at least 150% of the value deposited with a maturity date at least ten years in the future).

The average net return for the 150% Guaranteed Investment Account over the last six years would have been 22% a year. The average net return on the 100% Guaranteed Investment Account over the last six years would have been 27% a year. The average annual net return for The Winchester Life Umbrella Account over the last twelve years would have been 35% a year.

The minimum accounts accepted are $20,000 for The Winchester Life Umbrella Account, $20,000 for The Winchester Life 100% Guaranteed Account, and $50,000 for The Winchester Life 150% Guaranteed Account.

Although commodities are a speculative form of investment, investors everywhere are diversifying part of their portfolios to take part in the considerable potential profit opportunities that are available in the commodity, currency, precious metals and financial futures markets. The programs devised by the Dunn & Hargitt International Group will make profits if significant trends develop in either direction; i.e. up or down. This does not mean that short term results are always profitable, however the Dunn & Hargitt proven trading systems can provide above average returns over the longer term. Their objective is to make a profit for their clients of between 20% and 40% per annum and their computer trading systems are geared to this level of performance.

For more information, contact:

The Dunn & Hargitt International Group
c/o Dunn & Hargitt Research S.A.
Department S-697
P.O. Box 3186
Road Town, Tortola
British Virgin Islands

The structure of the Dunn & Hargitt Group has been established so that no taxes are withheld from the client's investment on the international commodity, currency, precious metals and financial futures markets. Because of this they can only manage money for investors who are neither citizens nor residents of the United States.

The Dunn & Hargitt International Group offers complete confidentiality to all of its clients, and will not reveal any information on a client or on its accounts to any third parties.

About the Author

This special afterword was prepared by Adam Starchild who over the past 25 years has been the author of over two dozen books, and hundreds of magazine articles, primarily on business and finance. His articles have appeared in a wide range of publications around the world — including *Business Credit, Euromoney, Finance, The Financial Planner, International Living, Offshore Financial Review, Reason, Tax Planning International, The Bull & Bear, Trust & Estates*, and many more.

Now semi-retired, he was the president of an international consulting group specializing in banking, finance and the development of new businesses, and director of a trust company.

Although this formidable testimony to expertise in his field, plus his current preoccupation with other books-in-progress, would not seem to leave time for a well-rounded existence, Starchild has won two Presidential Sports Awards and written several cookbooks, and is currently involved in a number of personal charitable projects.

His personal website is at http://www.adamstarchild.com

www.ingramcontent.com/pod-product-compliance
Lightning Source LLC
Chambersburg PA
CBHW051219200326
41519CB00025B/7177